Simplifying Coaching

Simplifying Coaching

How to have more transformational conversations by doing less

Claire Pedrick

Open University Press

Open University Press
McGraw Hill
8th Floor, 338 Euston Road
London
England
NW1 3BH

email: enquiries@openup.co.uk
world wide web: www.openup.co.uk

and Two Penn Plaza, New York, NY 10121-2289, USA

First edition published 2021

A catalogue record of this book is available from the British Library

ISBN-13: 9780335249077
ISBN-10: 0335249078
eISBN: 9780335249084

Library of Congress Cataloging-in-Publication Data
CIP data applied for
Printed and bound by CPI Group (UK) Ltd, Croydon, CR0 4YY

Typeset by Transforma Pvt. Ltd., Chennai, India

Praise page

"Claire stimulates a desire to know more about how to use existing skills in new and simplified ways. An altogether great book."
—*Clive Avril, Executive Coach and Mentor (ACC)*

"This is the kind of book that, after reading, you will want to have nearby for easy reference and reminders. I suspect that the well-worn pages will be a symbol of the book's lasting contribution to coaching – and to transformational conversations. A clear, concise summation of coaching that will benefit the new and the seasoned coach alike."
—*J. Val Hastings, MCC and President of Coaching4TodaysLeaders and Coaching4Clergy*

This book is dedicated to my Mum (1935–2020)

Contents

Preface

I am a coach. I have two learning laboratories. The first laboratory is over ten thousand hours of coaching conversations with a wonderful diversity of people; a few of these are working relationships built up over decades, and many are single sessions. The second laboratory is a privileged place where, for three or four days every week, I listen to people new to this approach coaching in training rooms on site and online, and where I supervise and mentor very experienced coaches. It is from eavesdropping on recordings of real conversations – my own and those of others – and observing against the International Coaching Federation (ICF) Coaching Competencies of Mastery that I have learned to simplify my practice. This is the simplicity that we teach.

Watching people respond to their coach's coaching, I have noticed that as the coach does less, I see transformation more often and more quickly. 3D Coaching, the company I founded in the late 1990s, has dropped the word coaching from most of its training. What was called *Coaching for Excellence* is now called *Transforming Conversations*. This craft – where people have insights about their own situation that will make a fundamental difference in their work and life – has an impact far beyond formal coaching.

Whether you aspire to be, or are already, a professional coach or someone who uses coaching at work, coaching is a process that works best when we get out of the way. Deep down in the coaching competencies of the ICF is a tiny but seismic phrase: '... *the coach trusts the process more than they trust themselves.*'[1] This conversation, relationship or engagement is an extraordinary process that has little to do with our ego, authority, models or power. The models aren't the bit that make coaching work.

This book is written for professional coaches working independently and in organisations, as well as students of coaching, leaders, managers who want to use a coaching style, ministers, mentors, healthcare workers, social prescribers, supervisors – in fact, anyone who shares a desire to have conversations with others that are useful and enable change to happen in individuals, teams, organisations or wider society.

Coaching is for everyone. Drawing from science, the learning lab, coaching competencies and common sense, *Simplifying Coaching* is about applying some tweaks that will make your conversations more productive and more likely to be transformational.

Everyone has some skill in listening, talking to others and asking questions. *Simplifying Coaching* is not another coaching model. It is an encouragement to do what you already do, more simply. Coaching is about people talking to people. For clarity, I will call the facilitator of the conversation the *coach*, and the person who is bringing their stuff the *thinker*. Nancy Kline first used the term thinker in 1999.[2] It is interesting how, twenty years later, the coaching industry has not followed suit and mostly uses the words client or coachee to describe the people we work with. More of that in Chapter 7.

If this is the first book you have picked up about coaching, it's an excellent place to start – simply. Whoever you are, you will find ways here to make your coaching more relaxed and more effective. *Simplifying Coaching* is about integrating learning and paying attention not only to what you know but how you do what you do. This is the art of coaching.

'*There is nothing new under the sun*' says the Book of Ecclesiastes.[3] I have tried to acknowledge everything that I have picked up from others and made my own. But there are also things that I have written that have been unconsciously absorbed or of which I am unaware of the origin. Much of this book has come from exploring with others what happens when you apply science to the art of the conversation. New learning has come when someone says, '*Make that simple*' and I have asked, '*What do we need to do to make that happen?*' Sometimes learning has come suddenly – like the insights about STOKeRS in Chapter 3. Or in a masterclass, where the deep learning about *being with* rather than *talking to* came from a diagram that someone emailed me after we had been learning together. I encourage you to make what you are learning your own, too.

Someone once said, '*if you can't explain it simply, you don't understand it well enough*' (this is commonly attributed to Einstein). I cannot teach you to make every conversation transformational. And working more simply means that we are less likely to miss transformation when it happens, because we are not so busy thinking about what to do next that we fail to see what is emerging.

I spend time with people who have qualified in coaching with a sturdy toolbox having never had coaching from an experienced coach. Nor have they observed coaching. All their learning is from the classroom, reading, practising with fellow students and writing reflections. They are often required to apply several tools or models in a conversation so that they can reflect on what they are learning. They are so overwhelmed that they cannot fully hear the person who has come for a conversation with them. Too much head knowledge can make for complex conversations. We work too hard. And when we do too much work, the person who has come to talk to us does less.

Several times a year, I am invited into public sector organisations to run 'return to coaching' workshops for people who have done accredited coach training and lost enthusiasm or confidence. They come because they are overwhelmed and tired. They arrive thinking that they are not applying what they learned because it needs to be utilised in a room, sitting down with the door shut. Formal coaching has its place. And there are some simple principles in coaching that can be applied alone or together to tweak almost every kind of conversation we have that will make them even more effective. However much we learn, and however many books we read, we cannot become an expert in having conversations with a thousand different types of people. We do not know how to make a conversation effective with anyone unless we ask them.

Coaching is a multi-million pound industry. It is not a dark art that we should keep secret because we can earn lots of money – although there is money to be made. Coaching is an art. It is special. And it is deeply simple. I want people to trust coaching as a useful process – whether they are brand new or executive coaches, whether they are having a quick conversation in the corridor or with someone who is paying. I want coaches to be confident, empowered and brave so that we can develop people who are confident, empowered and brave.

Many years ago, a lady called me to talk about having some coaching. She had been referred by a friend who knew me. She also spoke to a coach in Australia about the coaching programme he could offer her. She went for the shiny £1,000 programme. A year later, she met her friend who asked her whether she had moved forward with the question she had taken to coaching. She described all the processes and techniques they had been through. 'And your question?' asked our mutual friend. They had not addressed it. The lady called me and said she'd like to have some coaching and had run out of money. We had a quick chat, and I asked her a question based on what she was saying. Later she reported to her friend that the question had unlocked the place she was stuck in, and moved her forward. There is a lot written about coaching – this model, that technique. Claims that if you work with me, I can do this, that or the other. Great coaching is as much about the process as it is about you or me.

How to use this book

If you find it hard to believe that simple can be transformational, I invite you to suspend your disbelief and try out some of what you will find in the pages that follow. The principles here are simple. All of them will be things you sometimes do either consciously or intuitively. When conversations are less effective than you had hoped for, you may not be able to draw on the insights. Noticing them and naming them means that they become skills that you can draw on consciously. As much as they are about coaching, they have an application far wider in other conversations in the workplace, in family and friendship groups, and in our communities.

Read in an order that works for you. I hope that you will be inspired to integrate what you find useful as you tweak your conversations. This will simplify the work you do, make it more effective for those you work with, and help you sleep at night! I would like you to skip down the road after a conversation, while the person who has been doing their thinking needs to lie down in a dark room and continue to process their deep learning.

Please don't apply everything you like at the same time with the next person you coach!

Notes

1 International Coaching Federation, (2020) *ICF Core Competencies Rating Levels*, available at: www.coachfederation.org/app/uploads/2017/12/ICFCompetenciesLevels Table.pdf (accessed 27 March 2020).
2 Kline, N. (1999), *Time to Think: Listening to Ignite the Human Mind*, London: Ward Locke.
3 *Holy Bible – New International Version* (1986), London: Hodder & Stoughton.

Acknowledgements

It would take a whole book to name the people who every day have enabled the insights I will share here. Some did it by working simply – others by being complicated. Our learning emerged as we thought together about what might be a simpler and more effective way. Whether or not you are named here, I am deeply grateful to each one of you for the gift you have given:

All of the team at 3D Coaching – past, present and future – who through the years have wondered, shared and grown ideas with me.
Peronel Barnes for the diagrams.
My coach mentors and supervisors Ginny Baillie, Phil Brew and Fiona Adamson have travelled with me as I have gained in confidence to speak up that there must be a simpler way.
Aboodi Shabi whose wise counsel to move from courses to finding a teacher, to learn and to make things my own led me to all kinds of insights.
Vanessa Winstanley who introduced me to the word 'rightsizing' in a conversation about the final draft which has been a gift of simplicity.
The wise owls of the UK International Coaching Federation.
My Wisdom Circle.
And my teachers – Peter Hawkins, Nick Smith and John Whittington have all travelled with me as I have made this my own.
J. Val Hastings MCC is still my thinking and simplifying buddy.

My most significant learning has come from those I have coached and mentored and trained – especially those of you who have asked questions or pushed back.

Finally, I am grateful to my family, my stalwart administrator Sue Appleton, and to Mads, John and Lydia, whose living and dying taught me so much about the value of simple conversation.

Glossary

APECS	Association for Professional Executive Coaching and Supervision
CPD	Continuing Professional Development
EMCC	European Mentoring and Coaching Council
ICF	International Coaching Federation
Internal Coach	A coach employed by an organisation to coach colleagues
External Coach	A coach who does not work for the same organisation as the thinker

1 It's a journey

Why simple?

Writing about the evolution of aircraft design, pilot Antoine de Saint-Exupéry observed that '*in anything at all, perfection is finally attained not when there is no longer anything to add, but when there is no longer anything to take away*'.[1] Like perfection, simplifying requires taking things away. In the British TV show *MasterChef*, contestants cook under pressure in front of professional judges and receive robust feedback. The chefs who get to the final are the ones who are learning. This almost always invites them to use fewer ingredients in a dish and to season more with salt and pepper. As well as their latent talent, and a determination to succeed, it is continuously applying what they are learning about simplifying that enables them to excel in their craft.

If your job is to listen to – and talk with – people for more than half your working week, you are in conversations for about 1,000 hours every year at work. If you have been working for ten years, you have been doing that for about 10,000 hours. In that time, you will have developed a conversational style that works most of the time, and yet you may never get useful feedback. Colleagues will say it was useful if they like it. If they did not like it, they might tell someone else. That does not mean that the first conversation was helpful, and the second was not. When we move to a coaching style, as much as learning a different way, this will be influenced by where we were formed to have conversations.

Like progressing through *MasterChef*, improving the quality of any conversation means unlearning habits that have been well-formed over many years. Mastery in coaching, like excellence in cooking, comes from the wisdom of experience combined with a depth of simplicity. It is about practice. It is about making mistakes and learning from them. I may have many thousands of hours of coaching experience – but you can be an outstanding coach or colleague using a simple coaching approach from day one. I am learning all the time. Testing out some of the ideas for this book has challenged me to simplify even more.

Simple isn't easy

The journey to working simply is not easy. Eric Parsloe, one of the founders of the European Mentoring and Coaching Council (EMCC), used to dine out on saying that just because coaching is simple doesn't mean it is easy. Simplicity requires a significant amount of reduction and unlearning.[2] Not all the habits we have acquired are useful to others. The simplicity in aircraft design of which de Saint Exupéry spoke took several generations to refine.

Coaching is not new. Socrates was using something like coaching more than 2,000 years ago.[3] Yet it is interesting to notice that in my coaching lifetime, more is being brought in than is being taken away. The night before a coaching conference where I was doing a keynote called 'Deeply Simple', another speaker told me that a good word to describe my talk was 'simplexity'.[4] Within minutes of tweeting that simplexity was my subject, I received a private message which stated, *'Delete that tweet. You have been seduced by someone else's need to make the simple complex'*.

Simplifying is not dumbing down this precious, life-changing art of coaching. It is not shallow. In fact, working simply can go very deep. Simplifying coaching is learning how to do the least we need to do, in service of creating a safe, supportive and challenging[5] environment in which someone can think and do some useful work. In these conversations, it is what Hawkins and Smith (2012) describe as our presence (how people experience us in the room) that has as much impact as authority (what we know).[6] If we are to work in partnership with someone, we need to share the work. Doing more in conversations may give us worth and demonstrate our wisdom, but it does not necessarily add value. The value of a coaching conversation comes from what happens after it is over. Not just from what happens in the room.

Simplicity can look unimpressive. In a talk, the founder of *what3words*, a really simple global navigation tool, noticed that the tool had been well received by the public and that the tech world was somewhat underwhelmed. The tech world, however, are not the intended users.

The context in which we work has changed significantly since I started coaching in the 1980s. The world in which our conversations take place is more visibly volatile, complex, uncertain and ambiguous (Whiteman, 1998).[7] We don't have the control we think we have. That is well evidenced by the Covid-19 pandemic. If you match the complexity people bring with them with the complexity in our questions and the sheer volume of words, it will become clear that navigating a conversation is hard work for both parties. When you engage in complex thinking with simplicity, it is easier for them to see what is, more clearly. Offering a safe place to be still, to think simply and in a future-focused way is a gift.

Transformation

What, then, is transformation? In science, transformation is defined as *'the action of changing in form, shape, or appearance; metamorphosis'*.[8] Chemicals are combined with a catalyst in a test tube or conical flask, and the subsequent reaction means that they are changed. Scientific reactions can be permanent or reversible. Transformation happens in other places. In baking, ingredients are combined in a tin and heat is applied. A cake cannot revert to its original state. It is changed forever. The potential for transformation in people through building a container is described by Senge et al. as follows: *'just as the cauldron [in a steel refinery] contains the energies of molten steel, dialogue involves creating a container that can hold human energy, so that it can be transformative rather than destructive'.*[9]

Transactional conversations are useful. They produce insights around what to do next or how to do it. Transformation in people is *'a complete change in character'.*[10] Transformational insights are more profound and longer-lasting. They are more likely to be about character (who) than pragmatic action (what or how). Transformation is sometimes described as a light-bulb moment when someone sees or hears that something has changed significantly. Hawkins and Smith describe this as a *'shift in the room'.*[11] Moons recognises that this is the beginning of a deeper change because *'the insight itself will not lead to changed behaviour automatically'.*[12] It is an indicator of the beginning of transformation. The coach's role is to notice and ask, *'what do we need to do now?'* That can be as simple as: *'And now you know that?'*

We cannot make transformation happen. Inspired by Senge's insight into transformation with groups, I wondered what would happen if we applied this learning to a conversation. Is permanent change or transformation more likely to happen when the conversation is also in a container?

Co-creating the container

There is a Chinese proverb that says, *'The banks of the Yangtse give it depth, drive and direction'.* Without good boundaries, conversations – like rivers – can turn into floods or puddles. Co-creating a container for the conversation we are having puts in boundaries around it that will make it more likely to be transformational. When I am in conversation with someone, whether they are a colleague or someone who has hired me to be their coach, the only thing we can influence is what is in the container we have co-created today. This is what we are doing together here today in this room or virtual space. That's all we have in our gift together. And all that is in their gift is how they do what they do when they leave the room.

I like to call *'what we are doing today'* rightsizing. Rightsizing a conversation is a way to contain the conversation enough for us to be clear what we are doing today. You can put this container (Fig. 1) around any kind of coaching model. It simply means that we don't start doing the work until we know what we are doing.

Without a container, transformation might still happen, and it may take a while to get to the heart of the matter. Creating a container by rightsizing the conversation together enables you to work in partnership with the other person to create the beginning of the conversation. Then we do the work that gets to

Figure 1 The coaching container

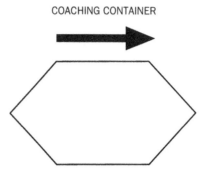

the heart of the matter more quickly. Finally, we close the conversation in partnership. That is easier for you and more effective for them.

Future-focused

In *The Psychology of Hope*,[13] positive psychologist Rick Snyder addresses *Will Power* – someone's will to shape their future, and *Way Power* – their ability to see ways to do that. A usually positive person can lack hope when they have the will power – they want to move forward – but have not yet found way power – they haven't yet worked out how to do so. A coaching style is a future-focused and safe space where they can begin to see how to find their way power. Creating the coaching container together is a way to start that process and a useful way of ensuring that the conversation is forward facing.

How to have more transformational conversations by doing less

Although you can replicate chemical transformation under laboratory conditions, there is no formula or strategy to make transformation happen in a conversation. Throughout this book, I will share with you some of what I have learnt about how to increase the potential for transformation. Most of this follows de Saint Exupéry's example of taking away and doing less.

There is a journey to be taken to doing less. We were formed in having conversations as children and in our early professional lives. My learning journey consciously began in the 1990s after reading an article in *Good Housekeeping* magazine about Thomas Leonard.[14] I realised that I had been coaching for more than ten years. My job title was 'Information and Counselling Secretary'. Everyone who came to see me for a conversation was looking at future possibilities. They wanted thinking space. When they had clarified what their question was about working in overseas development, they wanted ideas about where and how to access the information they would need to take the next step. At that time, counselling was the closest word that described the role. I now recognise that it was coaching and mentoring. After absorbing the fact that this thing I had been doing had a name that was becoming more widely used, I talked to a few coaches and signed up to professional coach training in order to formalise what I was already doing and to learn how to be even more effective in the role.

Four weeks after paying the fees, the postman arrived with a large box. There were five reams of handouts with sections on how to coach every kind of person, as well as plenty of material on developing the nuts and bolts of what happens in coaching sessions. I had the enthusiasm of the beginner. Over two decades later, I acknowledge that I had welcomed the idea that coaching is a special thing, and that becoming a trained and accredited coach would give me the skills to facilitate unique conversations. What do I know now? Coaching is extraordinary and very special. And it is also not special at all. It is simply a future-focused conversation that can happen everywhere and anywhere.

Too much '*knowledge … is power*'[15] said Francis Bacon in the sixteenth century. In Bacon's days, a journey to acquire knowledge would have been slow. Today a search on Google for coaching produces over one billion seven hundred and forty million hits. If you have a preference for knowledge, there is plenty of knowledge out there. And unless knowledge, skills and experience are in balance, the knowledge can be experienced as power.

Models and tools

One of our customers has a training room with a cupboard in the corner. It is large enough to hold two vans. Recently, they invited me to deliver the final day of an accredited coach training programme. There were a dozen delegates in an enormous room. They had learned a lot of things throughout their year's training through reading, written assignments and reflections, as well as practised coaching. This was their final day before they were signed off as organisational coaches. The lack of energy in the room was palpable. They were exhausted. I put two chairs at the front of the room. Sitting down on the coach's chair, I invited someone to sit in the thinking chair. '*How does it feel*', I asked the group, '*when you start a conversation with someone knowing that the cupboard over there represents your stash of models, useful questions and knowledge. And you can't remember the bit you really need?*' Now I had their attention. I looked at the person who had come to think with me, got off my chair and walked into the cupboard to – metaphorically – find a question. She had to wait for me.

Good practical coaching programmes develop robust coaching. Theory-heavy programmes develop tool-heavy coaching. What organisations need is people who can be supportive and challenging, who can hold their nerve and so hold the system. They might be required to deliver formal coaching sessions. And when they can adapt what they are learning, they can use it in five-minute coaching conversations with colleagues. That is where value is added for the organisation, and the culture begins to change.

Theories matter. *'Learn your theories as well as you can, but put them aside when you touch the miracle of the living soul'*, said Jung.[16] Coaching works when two souls are working in partnership together. Unless it is well integrated, knowing too much can be overwhelming. It becomes another party in the conversation and interrupts the flow. You begin listening to your knowledge as well as the person who has come to think, and they start to wait while you are working out what to do next. It is like dancing with the instruction book in your hand. If you are feeling overwhelmed by the process, you will not be as useful as you could be. You will be busy and not fully listening to them. The thinker is the primary source of what we need to do.

If you only teach people as much as they need to know to get started on this different way of having conversations, I notice that they are better at working in partnership than someone who starts with a large amount of knowledge. They can continue to learn theories over time if they are useful. Last year someone arrived at a Return to Coaching course thinking that she had signed up for an Introduction to Coaching. She had travelled a distance, so I invited her to stay. The day was about simplifying. By the end of the day, she had facilitated a conversation with someone who moved from being very stuck, to having some significant insights about how she could do her job in a way that was more life-giving to her. Not all trained coaches had the same experience. Many of them were doing too much of the work.

Everyone we talk with is unique. They each need something a little different. Every time we speak we need to make that conversation effective. Whatever knowledge we may have, none of us knows how to have a great conversation with this person today, unless we ask them. To ask them is the first principle of simplifying coaching.

Making meaning

I hated English Literature as a child. Now I love literature and poetry. Analysing poetry at school and annotating everything was a very different art from sitting with it now and allowing it to make its own meaning within me. When we give people space to think, they will think. Coaches sometimes poke. We work too hard. We interrupt thinkers thinking. Offering our meaning might provide us with insight. And it may be meaningless to them. Let's think about the least that we need to do so that they can make meaning for themselves. That is what enables transformation to happen.

It's confusing (or less is more)

We received a call from an insurance company that wanted to be sure that their internal coaching programme was compliant. They had chosen to benchmark their internal coaches against the International Coaching Federation

Competencies, and wanted a company who could help them do that. The Head of Learning and Development had spent the weekend doing an online supermarket sweep of coaching books, and had dipped into them all. He was confused. They contradicted each other. They were about doing more. Coaching mastery is about doing less. The shift to simplicity is about who does the talking and who does the work.

What is coaching?

In *The 7 Habits of Highly Effective People*, Stephen Covey advocates beginning *'with the end in mind'*.[17] Let's stay simple and start there. At the end of a conversation, we hope that the person we are talking with will have felt heard, have done some work and have some new insights into their own situation, behaviour and context that will make a difference to what they do or think or feel. They will move forward, and we hope that this movement will be transformational.

As soon as you talk about coaching, people go into the mindset that you are an expert. The dictionary definition of a coach is someone who *'trains others for an athletic contest, esp. a boat-race'* or *'a private tutor who prepares a candidate for an examination'*.[18] The first definition is about training, teaching or instructing in sport. The second is giving instructions or advice – for instance, coaching a witness. Both descriptions are about providing content or knowledge. It is interesting that the coaching profession feels mature and yet what we do has not made it into the dictionary at all. Keith Webb describes coaching simply as *'drawing out'* and mentoring as *'putting in'*.[19]

The UK's Chartered Institute of Personnel Development (CIPD) has produced some guidelines about coaching, describing it as:

- a non-directive form of development
- focusing on improving performance and an individual's development
- possibly being personal, but the emphasis is on work performance
- having both organisational and individual goals
- providing an opportunity for people to better assess their strengths as well as their development[20]

Recognising the skill involved, CIPD recommends that coaching is done by people who are trained – whether they are managers using a coaching style or trained coaches. However, their definition does not describe what happens in the room. Neither does that of the Association for Coaching, which talks about the coaching process over time as *'a collaborative solution-focused, results-orientated and systematic process in which the coach facilitates the enhancement of work performance, life experience, self-directed learning and personal growth of the coachee'*.[21] Although the International

Coach Federation (ICF) talks about partnership, their definition is also unclear about what happens in the room: *'Partnering with clients in a thought-provoking and creative process that inspires them to maximize their personal and professional potential'.*[22]

The EMCC describes the coaching process as *'a structured, purposeful and transformational process, helping clients to see and test alternative ways for improvement of competence, decision making and enhancement of quality of life'.*[23] The EMCC then begins to describe what happens in the room as follows:

> 'Coach and Mentor and client work together in a partnering relationship on strictly confidential terms. In this relationship, clients are experts on the content & decision-making level; the coach & mentor is an expert in professionally guiding the process'.

It is interesting how many words are used here to describe what is simply a future-focused conversation between two people working in partnership in service of the thinking of one of them. The thinker does some work that enables them to gain new insights that moves them forward – coaching is keeping them company while they think. The conversation happens through the partnership described by EMCC and ICF. Perhaps a better definition of a coach is a thinking partner.

Partnership is so important to the conversation, and the relationship, that Chapter 7 is dedicated to exploring what that looks like. For now, it is enough to say that coaching is about creating the right environment to do some work together. Unless that work is in partnership, our expertise can take precedence over the expertise of the unique individual with whom we engage with for a time. Everything we learn about coaching may be useful. And we may need very little of it. Perhaps the Ignatian description of *'bearing witness'*[24] gives a useful insight into what we are here to do.

Whatever your definition of coaching, the more work you do and the more words you use, the less space and time the thinker will have to do their work. That's pure mathematics. Once you have started explaining something, they are unlikely to interrupt. Now they are listening to us. Coaching is an opportunity for them to listen to and hear themselves. A useful stance is to ask ourselves: *'What's the least that we need to do together in order to enable new insight in this person?'*

Simplifying coaching is not reductionist, simplistic, or shallow. Like de Saint-Exupéry's view of aircraft design, the journey to becoming a great coach is about taking away words, tools and techniques, and doing less. If we are doing too much work in the conversation, we may need to unlearn some habits in order to make more space for the thinker to think. An executive coach who tried out this simplicity the day after some continuing professional development describes coaching more simply as *'an amazing gift to enable people to find their own wisdom'.*

What is coaching for?

People come to coaching for all kinds of reasons. In a supervision session, coach Adrian Goodall[25] and I noticed that people seem to come:

- with a thing to explore – doing something differently, or being different
- when they are stuck
- as they are transitioning into a new job or project
- to think about endings or beginnings
- because they need a place outside their context – family or organisation – where, over time, they would like an external thinking partner or critical friend
- because they have been sent
- for a reason they can't articulate

Some of these will require consistent and regular conversations over a few weeks or months, some might be done in one conversation, and some are relationships over a much longer period of time.

How many? How often? How long?

People using a coaching style at work just use it as and when it's useful. Coaches usually offer blocks of sessions for a standard length of time; often one or two hours for four to six or even up to twelve sessions. This is administratively convenient and financially rewarding for the coach. It is also an ethical dilemma because it prioritises what a good business model for the coach – or coaching company – is over what the thinker might find useful. One of the conveniences of a fixed number is that the quantity of coaching is often negotiated with a third-party sponsor before the thinker is involved at all.

Organisations with internal coaching programmes use a model for the number and frequency of sessions that is based on this financial and administrative model from external coaching. This has been around since my training in the late 1990s, when we were taught to see people four times a month for 45-minute sessions. This is aligned with a model of weekly therapy, and comes from the paradigm of coaching as helping. In the early days, we probably knew no better. Coaching is not therapy. If we believe that coaching is about people moving forwards and we are working transformationally, I hope that it will take more than a week to embed their insights from the last session. There will always be exceptions – for example, more frequent conversations might be required when coaching someone who is coming out of therapy and is taking small steps forward, or coaching a leader as they navigate their workplace through coronavirus. But generally, we should expect our coaching conversations to have more of a lasting impact than a week. If we know twelve sessions are planned, it is unlikely that every conversation will be transformational.

It is not only the thinker who is a casualty of any package that is imposed on them. An NHS coach expressed concern to me that her coaching was inadequate. Although their first conversation had moved all kinds of things forward, the colleague she was coaching showed no further progress in the next four sessions and was hesitant in booking their final meeting. When we talked, it was clear that the first session had done what was needed. That was enough. Sadly, respecting the organisation's package meant that the newly qualified coach lost confidence. Equally, the thinker became frustrated with the process that had been useful at first. This damaged the reputation of the coaching process and the confidence of the coach.

Bespoke

Whatever their reason for seeking coaching, every person's journey is unique. What the coaching needs to look like begins with knowing what the conversation(s) will be for. What is the question they are bringing? Until they have started doing some work with you, they will not know what coaching is like, and neither of you will know the best way for them to engage with it. This means that it is impossible to answer questions about how many sessions, how long or how often they should be, until you have started working together. This is inconvenient when you are working through a third party who is commissioning the work, whether that is an organisational sponsor or an associate company.

After one session, the reason for the coaching becomes clearer. You will both have a better sense as to whether the thinker needs time to process – in which case a more extended session will be useful; or whether they process quickly internally and would prefer to go and land their insights on their own – in which case a much shorter session may be useful. You may take time to establish the right pace and length. Being open to adapt this ensures that they can make the very best of the process.

Going slowly is not an indicator that coaching is not working. If you are going slowly, check in with yourself that this is coaching and that you are doing work together, and with them that they are moving forward. Retained coaching offers open access to you whenever they need a place to think. A sessional engagement works well for others. It is convenient and financially rewarding to offer packages. In retained coaching you charge for the relationship, not the time.

Single-session coaching

One conversation can be enough. Single-session coaching is a valid way of working for some people. It is effective when the thinker trusts the coaching process or the person who has recommended it to them. They come once. And they can come back again later if that's useful. Other people take longer to engage with the process.

A spare one

There will be times when it seems that we have done the work we need to do, and the thinker is hesitant about drawing the coaching process to a close. When I am coaching in organisations, I regularly end a series of conversations early when the work is done and hold a spare session in credit forever. This is a shift from sessional work to retained work. Although the suggestion of a session in hand is met with relief, it is rarely taken up because the thinker begins to recognise over time that they can engage with this themselves. They start to facilitate their own thinking.

Professional coaching bodies

There are many organisations in the coaching arena for independent external coaches, internal coaches – people who do coaching formally in their organisation – and managers and leaders who use a coaching style. At the time of writing, I am looking at the European Mentoring and Coaching Council (EMCC), the International Coach Federation (ICF) and the Association for Coaching, all of which have competency frameworks. I do not include the Association for Professional Executive Coaching and Supervision (APECS) because it *'uses a capability based framework (as opposed to competencies) to evaluate and acknowledge an executive coach's level of professional standing'*.[26] The APECS framework includes a combination of

- what you have done (past work experience)
- what you know (knowledge)
- what you do (models and techniques)

The EMCC and ICF describe different tiers of competency dependent on someone's experience, while the Association for Coaching has one set for all coaches. The EMCC and ICF indicators of a higher level of capability – Master Practitioner (EMCC) and Master Certified Coach (ICF) – describe a simpler practice and more presence than the Foundation and Associate Credentialed Coach descriptors.

What enables conversations to be transformational, I think, is not work experience, knowledge or models, although they might be useful. What matters most is how we do what we do in coaching conversations. This is about presence and practice. In Chapter 7 we will explore partnership and why it is fundamental to great coaching. Too much theory, too early, combined with too little practical experience can overwhelm both coach and thinker.

My experience is that you can teach the competencies of mastery to beginners without going through all the models and techniques. This is not a new concept. My daughters learned from their driving instructor's wisdom to change from second to fourth gear in a manual (stick shift) car. Thirty years before, my instructor had drilled me into going up and down the gears sequentially come what may. Like passing your driving test, completing a coaching course does not bring with it the wisdom that comes with experience. But working simply is a good start.

The competency frameworks provide some great insights for professional practice when they are held simply. Somewhere between the coaching competencies and the coaching room lie the training providers. It is important to acknowledge honestly that their interest is commercial as well as educational.

The heart of the matter

The journey to simplicity requires some unlearning and doing less so that the person we are with does as much of the work as possible as we keep them company in their processing and ask questions only when it is useful to them.

People come to coaching because they are on a journey. The journey belongs to them. We are their companions from time to time. Much of the time they travel independently. Some people have chosen to make the journey, others have been sent. Coaching simply is about doing the least we need to do to enable them to travel well. It is a conversation which serves the individual with whom we are talking, and the systems which they inhabit: their family, team, organisation and/or society. The heart of our work is simply to serve the unique human being who is in conversation with us by co-creating a conversation, or series of conversations, which are useful to them. They are the expert in their own lives. What we do, or how we perform, is in service of them.

Mastery, says the ICF, is demonstrated when '*the coach evidences a complete curiosity that is undiluted by a need to perform; the coach is in fully partnered conversation with client [thinker]; [and] the coach trusts that value is inherent in the process versus having any need to create value*'.[27] Great coaching is not about us!

Notes

1 de Saint Exupéry, A. (1939), *Wind, Sand and Stars*, trans. L. Galantiére, New York: Reynal & Hitchcock.
2 Wilkinson, D. (2018), *The Oxford Review research-based guide to unlearning*, available at: www.oxford-review.com/blog-unlearning-latest-research/ (accessed 18 March 2020).
3 Paul, R. and Elder, L. (2016), *The Thinker's Guide to Socratic Questioning* (Thinker's Guide Library), Dillon Beach, CA: Foundation for Critical Thinking.
4 Kluger, J. (2008), *Simplexity: Why Simple Things Become Complex (and How Complex Things Can Be Made Simple)*, New York: Hyperion.

5 Blakey, J. and Day, I. (2012), *Challenging Coaching: Going Beyond Traditional Coaching to Face the FACTS*, London: Nicholas Brealey.

6 Hawkins, P. and Smith, N. (2013), *Coaching, Mentoring and Organizational Consultancy: Supervision, Skills and Development*, 2nd edition, Maidenhead: Open University Press.

7 Whiteman, W. (1998), *Training and Educating Army Officers for the 21ˢᵗ Century*, Carlisle, PA: US Army War College Publications.

8 OED Online (March 2020), Oxford University Press, available at: https://www.oed.com/view/Entry/204743?redirectedFrom=transformation#eid (accessed 1 April 2020).

9 Senge, P., Sharmer, C.O., Jaworski, J. and Flowers, B. (2005), *Presence*, London: Nicholas Brealey.

10 OED Online (March 2020), Oxford University Press, available at: https://www.oed.com/view/Entry/204743?redirectedFrom=transformation#eid (accessed 1 April 2020).

11 Hawkins, P. and Smith, N. (2013), *Coaching, Mentoring and Organizational Consultancy: Supervision, Skills and Development*, 2nd edition, Maidenhead: Open University Press.

12 Moons, J. (2016), 'A shift in the room – myth or magic? How do coaches create transformational shifts in a short period of time?', *International Journal of Evidence Based Coaching and Mentoring*, Special Issue #10: 45–58, at p. 53.

13 Snyder, R. (1994), *The Psychology of Hope: You Can Get There From Here*, New York: Free Press.

14 Brock, V. (2009), *Coaching pioneers: Laura Whitworth and Thomas Leonard*, available at: https://researchportal.coachfederation.org/Document/Pdf/2966.pdf (accessed 1 April 2020)

15 Bacon, F. (1597), *Meditationes sacrae*, Londini: Excusum impensis Humfredi Hooper.

16 Quoted in Palmer, S. and Woolfe, R. (1999), *Integrative and Eclectic Counselling and Psychotherapy*, London: Sage.

17 Covey, S. (1999), *The 7 Habits of Highly Effective People*, New York: Simon & Schuster.

18 OED Online (March 2020), Oxford University Press, available at: https://www.oed.com/view/Entry/204743?redirectedFrom=transformation#eid (accessed 1 April 2020).

19 https://keithwebb.com with permission.

20 Chartered Institute of Personnel Development (CIPD) (2019), *Coaching and Mentoring*, available at: www.cipd.co.uk/knowledge/fundamentals/people/development/coaching-mentoring-factsheet (accessed 27 March 2020).

21 Association for Coaching (undated), *Coaching Defined*, available at: www.associationforcoaching.com/page/CoachingDefined (accessed 27 March 2020).

22 International Coaching Federation (ICF) (2020), *About ICF*, available at: https://coachfederation.org/about (accessed 19 March 2020).

23 European Mentoring and Coaching Council (EMCC) (2018), *EMCC Competence Framework Glossary*, revised, available at https://emccuk.org/Public/Professional_Development/Competence_Framework/Public/1Resources/Competence_Framework.aspx?hkey=ad98bd86-8bb8-4435-913d-5258f6774375 (accessed 19 March 2020).

24 Ivens, M., trans. (2004), *The Spiritual Exercises of Saint Ignatius of Loyola*, Leominster: Gracewing Publishing. In the spirit of the Second Annotation of the Spiritual Exercises.

25 With permission.

26 Association for Professional Executive Coaching and Supervision (APECS) (2020), available at: www.apecs.org (accessed 27 March 2020).

27 International Coaching Federation (ICF) (2020), *ICF Core Competencies Rating Levels*, available at: www.coachfederation.org/app/uploads/2017/12/ICFCompetencies LevelsTable.pdf (accessed 27 March 2020).

2 Simple listening: Notice, don't diagnose

What the coaching bodies say

There is agreement that listening is a core skill. The ICF states that the coach *'Listens actively: Focuses on what the client is and is not saying to fully understand what is being communicated in the context of the client systems and to support client self-expression'*.[1] The Association for Coaching is broadly in agreement, as the coach *'Demonstrates effective listening and clarifying skills and differentiates between what is said and what's left unsaid'*.[2] This implies deeply noticing, but a coach who *'identifies patterns of client thinking and actions'* (EMCC), seems to introduce the idea that the coach is there to make connections. The EMCC broadens noticing to be *'alert to tone and modularity as well as to explicit content of communication'*.[3] This is similar to the ICF, which invites coaches to *'notice[s], acknowledge[s] and explore[s] the client's emotions, energy shifts, non-verbal cues or other behaviours'*.[4]

A former colleague, Jeremy Clare, used to say that *'everyone needs a good listening to'*. Listening well is one of the greatest gifts we can give to another person. It is a skill developed in the womb and a fundamental life skill. Children might be told to listen, but they are taught how to listen much less than they are taught how to read, write or do mathematics. We inhabit a world that feels like it is on transmit. It is a fantasy that the opposite of transmitting words is listening. It is not. It is waiting to talk.

What is listening for?

As we sit with another human being, what is listening for? We listen so that the thinker feels heard by someone else, and so that they listen to themselves. We listen so that they can make new meaning for themselves and gain new insights and understanding into their own situation and context.

Coaching is different from other conversations. This extreme listening can transform the way people think and act as they begin to think about things in a new way. It is not a way for us to gather more information about the other. It is not a diagnosis, problem-solving, saving or interrogating. Too much information in the space between us makes us look more like an expert than a coach. After all, what are we going to do with the information once we have it? Data-gathering can skew the partnership that makes coaching effective. Too much information can tempt us to form opinions or solutions in our heads. Remember that when the thinker leaves at the end of a conversation, or a series of conversations, the data belongs to them. We will, hopefully, have learned something new about the coaching process, but we do not need research notes for their biography! For coaching to be effective, we will only need as much data in the room as is useful for the thinker. For some people that will mean that they bring in a lot of story. For others, it will be very little. Not being a mind reader, the only way for us to know how much is useful is to ask them: *'How much of the story is it useful for you to tell?'*

Listening differently

I sometimes wonder whether people are attracted to certain careers because of the way they listen – and whether they are formed to listen in their first career. The CEO who listens for direction and to fix; the physician who listens to diagnose; the lawyer who listens for evidence; the plumber who listens for the source of the problem; the child who listens for a way to get you to say 'yes'; the safety manager who listens to investigate the incident; the problem solver who listens to find the solution; the optimist who listens for hope; the conversationalist who listens to find a way of making their contribution to the dialogue; the inquisitive who listen to the story to get more interesting information; the coach who listens until their passion for what they are hearing gets in the way. At a party, we might listen for a way to join in the conversation – *'I've been on holiday there too – how did you find it?'*

In the consulting room, we want the doctor to work out what's wrong with us and propose a solution. They are experts in bodies, and we want a diagnosis. But when we are talking through a challenge with colleagues, and hear: *'The problem is this and here is what you should do'*, there is a subtle implication they think we can't, with thinking space, work out for ourselves what's going on. The diagnosis of the problem is swiftly followed by a solution. As much as the intention of this is to be helpful, the outcome is disempowering if a solution was not what you wanted. We are inquisitive human beings. Even amongst the most experienced coaches, silencing our internal, inherent tendency to diagnosis and prescription is a learning journey.

The closer that the discipline where you have been formed is to coaching, the harder it can be to listen in a slightly different way. If coaching is a conversation where someone feels heard and gets new insights they did not have before, then we are listening so that they understand more about their own stuff – not so that we understand. For many people moving towards a coaching style, this is a new behaviour that takes practice and duck tape. When we listen for something, we are not actually hearing all of what the other person is saying. When we make meaning as we listen, we stop listening. When we do this, our personal sieve is holding the things we are listening for and letting the rest go through. Listening so that they can understand happens at a deeper level and is more powerful.

A fundamental part of a coaching style is to listen so that the thinker can explore. When we do this, the insights that emerge are in service of the thinker. They are not for us. Working together so that they hear and see these for themselves is one of the greatest gifts we bring to coaching. This is where transformation happens. Active listening is active for both of us. For this to happen, we need enough space to notice.

Noticing

After more than thirty years of driving a manual (stick shift) car, we acquired an automatic. It was hard to drive differently. Early on there were several times when I tried to change gear with the brake, until I learned to perch my left leg right out of the way (thanks to a tip from someone in the back). Now I can switch between cars without a problem. Like the gear shift, when you have listened to how you normally listen for many years, it will take time to learn a different way. I will call this different way of listening noticing.

Reflecting back

Carl Rogers[5] said that for someone to feel heard, we need to reflect back to them and clarify what they have said to us. When they know what they said, our précis of their words may not add much value. And if you don't know what you think until you speak, the précis may be about giving insight to you, not to them.

People come to conversations wanting to see the wood, or the forest, for the trees. The person is so involved in the details that they have lost sight of the important things. They will talk in loops, circles and tangents as information, facts and feelings tumble out. They may be telling you a story which they have told themselves and others many times. If you are unsure whether they are thinking or simply telling you what they know already, ask them. If you are talking with a storyteller who repeats the same story to many people with seemingly no new insights, ask them: '*Have you told this to other people? I'm wondering, what will be different for you at the end of this conversation ...?*'

Following the complexity of what someone is saying at 150 words a minute is hard work for you, and you are at risk of getting lost in the tangle with them (Fig. 2). Reflecting back by clarifying or paraphrasing might enable them to feel heard and it will not always give them new insight. I know that because several days a week I do a listening exercise

Figure 2 How people speak

HEADLINES

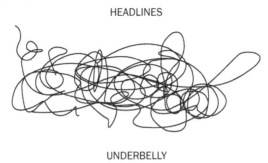

UNDERBELLY

in training rooms and ask them. It is unusual to have anyone get new insight from reflecting back alone.

Headlines

Headlines are the top notes of what is being said. The themes.

> Example: '*I have moved house twice in the last six months, lived in Asia and Europe, been promoted at work into a new team with a new direc-tor and one of my four children, Charlie, has had lots of problems at school. I'm so stressed I don't know which way is up!*'

Traditional paraphrasing or reflecting back says: '*You've moved house, in Asia and Europe, been promoted, your son has problems at school, and you're stressed?*' They feel heard. Unless Charlie is a girl, at which point, the flow of the conversation may well be disrupted as you apologise for your mistake. It is unlikely that these words give them new insight.

Listen differently, and you will notice some themes above the story. These are like newspaper headlines. Reflecting the headlines back to the thinker in a few words can be even more powerful than reflecting word for word. This is not a summary, and you may not be right – so the words always need to be in the form of a question: '*Several transitions? Lots to focus on?*' If you are wrong, the thinker will make the themes their own. This can bring insights. Headlines also make excellent short questions – more of that in Chapter 4.

Underbelly

Underneath the stories are emotions which we can hear through tone, pace, volume and the words that are used – or not used. These include feelings. Naming what we think the feelings are risks being diagnostic. We might be wrong, so always offer a question:

> Example: *'Lots of emotion?'*
> *'Stretched?'*
> *'Courage?'*

I call this underbelly. In nature, the underbelly of an animal is the soft abdomen that is more vulnerable than the tougher skin of their upper body. This represents the feelings underneath what is being said. Reflecting back the underbelly might be as simple as saying: *'It sounds like there's some emotion there'*. Even more powerful can be reflecting back as few of their exact words as possible – as a question: *'I'm so stressed?'*

When I do this exercise in the training room, there are often moist eyes as the person who has told their story receives the underbelly and gets an insight. Almost every time, the person who has noticed and offered it as a one-word question goes on to explain where the word they have chosen came from. The thinker's processing is interrupted by the volume of words, and the moment of insight is minimised. Less is more. Notice and wait!

Bravery, not control, is at the heart of great conversations. You may not know what you noticed until you begin speaking. Be brave: *'Something about?...'* If coaching is a conversation where someone feels heard and gains new insight, even the listening phase that comes at the beginning of a conversation can be useful when we listen differently. It is more than scene-setting. The work has already begun.

Popcorn moments

We are listening not so that we understand, but so that the thinker understands. I observed a group practising their coaching skills where the thinker had brought a question about what they were going to do about a holiday property. The coach had clearly asked a backwards-looking question about the location because when I arrived, the thinker was in full flow talking about the impact on the site of European history in the twentieth century. As I walked up to them, one of the group laughed: *'We look like we are at the cinema watching a very interesting film'*. They named this trance-like state a popcorn moment. Coaches can easily get into popcorn moments when the story is interesting. Great coaching is full of incomplete stories. It can be frustrating for us not to get the whole story when we are listening, but the conversation is not about us. We won't necessarily leave having heard all the facts that would be interesting to know. Some of the thinker's processing will happen silently inside their head. In fact, some people are grateful when we stop expecting them to tell us everything. Transformation comes when they make their own meaning – not when we make it for them.

The ICF states that great coaches '*demonstrate[s] curiosity during the coaching process*'.[6] I disagree. Great coaching is about enabling the thinker to be curious, not you. Over-curiosity, like over-helping, is a useful subject to take to coaching supervision or mentoring.

Listen to themselves

Partnership is not about us doing all the listening. Our role is to enable the thinker to listen to themselves and understand things in a new way. Professor Jose Luis Villegas Castellanos[7] found that people who talked out loud to think through mathematics problems were able to solve them faster and had more chance of arriving at the right answer. This is true in coaching for people who are tackling any type of problem. Saying things out loud helps people to hear themselves, and through hearing, they can reach a level of understanding that might not otherwise have been possible. For some people, being heard is enough. Your role might simply be to notice or ask them: '*Do you need to say that out loud?*'

Notice, don't diagnose

Noticing is more than listening. It is saying what we see and hear and sense without diagnosis, judgement or interpretation. What we sense may be intuition, emphasis, or what is unsaid. What we notice is most useful when it is

- short without any unnecessary padding
- asked with a question mark – we might be wrong
- based on real observable data

This takes practice. Every day, when people talk to me about situations, the first version almost always includes judgement. I may need to ask '*And what did you see?*' four or five times to get away from interpretation. Saying what you see, with a question mark, is a very powerful question.

Noticing well and without judgement takes vigilance. There is always more to learn. Some people have thinking faces that could easily be interpreted as angry. I can remember being in a room of about fifty people. Forty-nine were fully engaged, and one was watching me with a furrowed brow. Everywhere I moved, I caught sight of her face. My paranoia rose. At the end of the workshop, everyone left, and the person with the furrowed brow came up to me. By now, I had decided that she hated the training. And that she hated it so much she was going to complain to the sponsor. '*I loved that*', she said, '*it is my plan to stop training from PowerPoint and to learn with the room. Can we talk more about how you did that?*' Clearly, I had made a diagnosis.

Noticing real data is an art. Argyris[8] described noticing real data in his ladder of inference. He observed that as people set out what is happening in their world, they come with a mixture of

- real objective data: what they see
- selected data: a more subjective selection
- meaning affixed to the parts they have selected
- assumptions based on that selection
- conclusions drawn from the assumptions
- core beliefs developed from the conclusions
- actions they take on what they now believe to be true

In a heartbeat we have moved from real data to fantasy. Here is what happened in the writing of this book:

- Laura, my editor, had a meeting about the book in August. I asked her to text me the outcome. The day of the meeting I did not receive a text (real objective data).
- I decide that Laura did not send me a text (selected data).
- I think that Laura did not send me a text because the Press had decided not to accept my proposal (meaning affixed to the parts they have selected).
- I assume that my proposal was not good enough (assumptions based on that selection).
- I conclude that I had written it badly (conclusions drawn from the assumptions).
- I believe now that I have nothing to say about coaching (core beliefs developed from the conclusions).
- Fortunately I was on holiday, otherwise I might have lost confidence in my coaching and training (actions they take on what they now believe to be true).

In fact, Laura had emailed me, and because I was on holiday, I missed the message. You will have examples of your own. We are human, and we leap up the ladder of inference in seconds. The challenge in coaching is that we are two people. We may leap up the same ladder – or indeed a different one of our own. That is why noticing matters, and we need to pay the most attention to real observable data.

As a trainer for over twenty years, it has been a revelation to realise quite recently that when we train people to listen, we are almost always training them to ask questions at the same time. In this environment, they focus more on the quality of their questions than the art of listening. That is where they feel they will be judged. Great noticing is at the heart of great coaching. When we are training coaches, we include a 'noticer' in our quad practice. From the noticing chair, we can learn to simply notice at a deeper and more useful level. Sitting far enough away that you cannot hear what is being said escalates the learning. Noticers begin by being amateur analysts – noticing every nuance of movement and attaching meaning to it. For me, body language analysis is another place where we can inadvertently make ourselves the expert in someone else's life, which can skew the partnership that is the foundation of great coaching. Noticing means paying full attention to what we see and hear and sense. Without making meaning.

We can never be entirely clean in our coaching, even when we use Grove's Clean Language.[9] We will always notice with some bias. The more we work with real observable data, the more we can keep that under control. Bias is something to take to supervision. Goleman, in the form of R.D. Laing, said: *'the range of what we think and do is limited by what we fail to notice. And because we fail to notice that we fail to notice, there is little we can do to change; until we notice how failing to notice shapes our thoughts and deeds'.*[10]

Don't look away

As much as our role is to be a catalyst and a companion, it is also to bear witness to the conversation the thinker is having with themselves. This means we need to notice when transformation happens. In every culture I have worked in so far, you can see in someone's eyes when they have new insights. They may look away. There may be tiny movements in the skin next to the eyes. The delight of working simply is that it's not for us to make meaning of that. Simply notice – and ask: *'And the insight?'* If we mis-noticed, we can move on and have barely interrupted the thinking of our colleague.

I observe coaches respectfully look away when the thinker is thinking. I am not advocating staring people out but when they are thinking deeply they are often not looking at us. When we look away, we miss the transformation. They may not have noticed it happening themselves and it is for us to gently ask. Listening like this helps us get the pace of the conversation right, too. While they are not looking at us, they probably don't want us to speak!

Note-taking

Many people find it useful to take notes when they are listening. If you are training as a coach, there may be an expectation that you take notes. The EMCC advocates *'keeping appropriate notes to track and review client progress with the client'*, although they don't say whether that is during the session or afterwards. Note-taking impacts the quality of your noticing. You are not looking. Also, the thinker may engage with you as they engage with other people who take notes. Coaching is different from other conversations, so it needs to look different.

> The group in the room happened to be mostly psychiatrists trained as internal coaches. As they began to practise in small groups, I watched them with their pens and paper in hand and had an overwhelming sense that what I saw was very close to what I would see in the psychiatrist's chair. What are notes for? In the medical world, they are to take a case history and symptoms, to record the diagnosis and treatment, and probably to protect against an investigation. When we take notes, are we slipping into a medical model that hyper-focuses on the problem? When someone is in the thinking chair, and it feels as though it is in the psychiatrist's chair, or the hospital consultant's room, or indeed the counselling chair, that is likely to affect their behaviour. Note-taking will impact both of you.

A coach I supervise used to take copious notes 'to find the challenge place'. She recognises now that she was missing the challenge places because she was looking in the wrong place. Pen and paper are a great tool in conversations. Give them to the thinker! If you are attached to note-taking, try reducing the size of your paper and using a tiny sticky note to capture what you need to retain – for example, when they keep using the same word.

Applying noticing at work

- Practise noticing what you see without putting in commentary.
- In meetings where you have significant amounts of time when others are presenting or speaking, notice headlines and underbelly.
- You'll have valuable insights if you choose to share what you are noticing.
- When you hear yourself, in other conversations, talking about something or someone, notice whether it is 'pure' observable data – and if it is not, ask yourself again – what did I see?
- If you need to write any kind of report about colleagues, saying what you see without judgement will serve you, and them, well as you source real objective data and begin to discard what is subjective.

What will you do differently at work as a result of what you have read in this chapter?

Applying noticing for experienced coaches

- Remember that the listening and noticing is not all our responsibility. Work even less hard – ask the thinker – what are the headlines? Or what do you notice?

- With permission, record some of your conversations and listen back, even if you don't like to listen to your own voice. You don't have to. The focus is to listen again to the thinker with the question: 'What am I noticing now that I am not feeling the pressure to form questions?' This is a very useful way of learning more deeply about your own timing, pace and space.
- Virtual coaching – it's possible to notice at this depth in any real-time live conversation whether that is face to face, video or audio only. Although coaching questions can be useful in an exchange of asynchronous messages, for example coaching by email, the lack of noticing real data will mean that less value is gained.
- A self-supervision question from coach Ian Mitchell: 'Do I notice what I'm noticing when I notice?'[11]

What will you do differently in your coaching as a result of what you have read in this chapter?

Applying noticing for coaching supervisors

In Hawkins and Shohet's Seven Eyed Supervision model,[12] Mode 1 is about real data – what did you see? As a coaching supervisor, I now ask those I supervise to bring along a recording at least once a year, so that we can see and notice what we notice together.

What will you do differently in supervision as a result of what you have read in this chapter?

Notes

1 International Coaching Federation (ICF) (2019), *Updated ICF Core Competency Model*, October, available at: https://coachfederation.org/app/uploads/2019/11/ICF-CompetencyModel_Oct2019.pdf (accessed 18 March 2020).

2 Association for Coaching (2012), *AC Coaching Competency Framework*, revised June 2012, available at: https://cdn.ymaws.com/www.associationforcoaching.com/resource/resmgr/accreditation/rclac/supporting_documenation/coaching_competency_framewor.pdf (accessed 27 March 2020).

3 European Mentoring and Coaching Council (EMCC) (2015), *EMCC Competence Framework V2*, September, available at: https://emccuk.org/Public/Professional_Development/Competence_Framework/Public/1Resources/Competence_Framework.aspx?hkey=ad98bd86-8bb8-4435-913d-5258f6774375 (accessed 19 March 2020).

4 International Coaching Federation (ICF) (2019), *Updated ICF Core Competency Model*, October, available at: https://coachfederation.org/app/uploads/2019/11/ICFCompetencyModel_Oct2019.pdf (accessed 18 March 2020).

5 Rogers, C. (1951), *Client-Centered Therapy: Its Current Practice, Implications and Theory*, London: Constable.

6 International Coaching Federation (ICF) (2019), *Updated ICF Core Competency Model*, October, available at: https://coachfederation.org/app/uploads/2019/11/ICF-CompetencyModel_Oct2019.pdf (accessed 18 March 2020).

7 Alleyne, R. (2009), 'Thinking out loud helps solve problems', *The Telegraph*, 22 December, available at: www.telegraph.co.uk/news/science/science-news/6866135/Thinking-out-loud-helps-solve-problems (accessed 27 March 2020).

8 Argyris, C. (1976), *Increasing Leadership Effectiveness*, New York: Wiley. Cited in Senge, P. (2006), *The Fifth Discipline: The Art and Practice of the Learning Organization*, revised edition, London: Doubleday.

9 Sullivan, W. and Rees, J. (2008), *Clean Language: Revealing Metaphors and Opening Minds*, Bancyfelin: Crown House Publishing.

10 Goleman, D. (1998), *Vital Lies, Simple Truths: The Psychology of Self-Deception*, London: Bloomsbury.

11 Via Twitter, with permission.

12 Hawkins, P. and Shohet, R., (2006), *Supervision in the Helping Professions*, 3rd edition, Maidenhead: Open University Press.

3 Simple beginnings

What the coaching bodies say

The professional bodies talk about careful contracting for the beginning of the relationship and the whole coaching engagement. They mention clarity on confidentiality, how many sessions, how often, good negotiations with stakeholders, etc. The ICF explicitly talks about establishing the coaching agreement at the beginning of every session where the coach will *'partner with the client … to: identify or reconfirm what they want to accomplish [today] … measures of success for [today] … manage the time and focus of [today] and continue coaching in the direction of the client's desired outcome unless the client indicates otherwise'.*[1]

Taking off the plane

On 25 March 2019,[2] a British Airways plane scheduled to travel from London to Düsseldorf flew to Edinburgh. Instead of heading east over the English Channel, the pilot headed north to the Scottish capital. No one noticed until he announced, *'Welcome to Edinburgh'*. The press report that when the crew and passengers said they had expected to be in Germany, the pilot asked the passengers to raise their hands if they had wanted to go to Düsseldorf. A passenger tweeted to the airline: *'While an interesting concept, I don't think anyone on board has signed up for this mystery travel lottery'*. For whatever reason, the pilot had set off towards Scotland. This was not a great beginning for anyone. They had arrived in a place they did not want to go.

The habits we have developed in one-to-one conversations are useful for some people who come to speak with us, and without much value for others. Our conversations may take them somewhere they have been before, to somewhere new or to a mystery destination. No one knows how to have a useful conversation with anyone at this time and in this place unless we ask them. Conversations can easily turn into the British Airways mystery tour when the person with the perceived power takes the lead and has not asked where we are going. When the thinker perceives us to have the power, they may not tell us if the conversation is not going where they need it to go.

Whether you open conversations in the same way every time, are loyal to where you have trained or start where you feel is useful, the opening moments of every encounter will set the tone. If coaching is to be different from other conversations, it needs to feel different from the start. We are here to do some work together that will be useful to the thinker. Mastery in coaching, says the ICF, is about beginning every conversation in full partnership.[3] This means co-creating where we are going today and checking in regularly that we are on track. If the pilot of flight BA3271 had asked that to the co-pilot, they might have noticed that the plane had not flown over the North Sea.

Beginning the conversation well is commonly known as contracting. And contracting is also a description of the business relationship. It is about confidentiality and logistics – how much, how many, how often shall we meet? It is also about the goal for the work – what are we here for?

In a conversation, a contract – or good take-off – is to agree together what we are doing today, how we will do it today and how we will know at the end of this conversation that we have done it. That happens in every conversation so that each time we make the work the right size for the time available. It simplifies and enables every conversation to be a more explicit partnership from start to finish.

Creating the coaching container

We need to co-create a new container (Fig. 1) every time we meet. This demonstrates true partnership. And the boundaries of the container means that the conversation is more likely to be transformational. Even if they found the last session useful, we don't know what will be useful to the thinker today unless we ask them. We are rightsizing what we are going to do together today. This agreement will probably change mid-conversation, but co-creating the container is an important step in establishing a culture that this is their conversation, and we are here to work in service of their thinking. It enables us to start somewhere that is useful to them.

As we do this, we might agree that we have no idea what we are doing and that we will work in a free-form and unbounded way today. This has still rightsized the work. If it is your preference to have no boundaries and go into open space today and see what happens, you are being directive unless you have decided that between you. Most people will answer the questions they are asked. They will follow you into the open space whether that is useful to them or not. Even if you are using the very best open questions, you are being directive if it was your decision alone to work in that way.

Rightsizing the container for today's conversation must include talking about time. It is a fantasy that you have all the time in the world. Being explicit is not suggesting that you do not value them. A container needs to have a boundary round the start and the end. Talking about time matters.

Coaching is different from other conversations. It is future-focused and optimistic and sets an expectation that things will change. Rightsizing every conversation means that you will get to the heart of the matter more quickly. Doing this well begins to move the thinker forward.

Perhaps Einstein was describing rightsizing when he said, '*if I had an hour to solve a problem, I'd spend 55 minutes thinking about the problem and 5 minutes thinking about the solution*'.[4] Einstein's language of problems and solutions has led to unrealistic expectations on the part of coaches and thinkers. Coaching is not about the coach solving someone else's problem. When our conversation is over, they will still need to take some kind of action to put their insights into practice. In the research behind *The Progress Principle*,[5] Amabile and Kramer discovered that when people start moving forward in their thinking, they keep moving. What we are doing is enabling them to get enough of a shift in perspective that their thinking begins to move. Any progress is progress.

If we change Einstein's words from '*What is your problem, or issue?*' to '*What is your question for today?*', the thinker starts to think. Movement has begun. So creating the coaching container well rightsizes the question to find the part that we need to explore together today. Suddenly we are both less overwhelmed. Questions don't need a solution. They evolve. If the thinker leaves the conversation with more clarity about their question, they will have begun to move forward.

STOKeRS

Taking time over the beginning of the conversation means that we don't start doing the work before we are clear what we are doing together today. It enables the thinker to work out what our focus needs to be without either of us getting lost in words. Rightsizing, or contracting, is not shallow. Depth comes as we engage, and push and challenge, and the contract will often be changed later in the conversation. We have to start somewhere. Here is an example of some questions that co-create the container and rightsize the question. They are built out of the ICF competencies for establishing the coaching agreement in every conversation.

SUBJECT: *'What would you like to think about today?'*

We are meeting to do some work together today in service of the thinker exploring, thinking, processing and developing new ideas and insights. If this is going to be different from other conversations they have, we need to use different language. When we ask them what they would like to bring, to talk about or discuss, there's a risk that this could become more about talking around the thing that they bring than about agreeing what to do with it now it has been brought. If you avoid '*How can I help you?*' questions in coaching, you are demonstrating that coaching is different.

It is unusual for someone to come to a conversation with a question that is manageable in the time we have. When I listen to people coaching, I hear them dive into the heart of the conversation after their opening question. Unless we work out together which bit of the question is important or useful, we may get lost together. Everything the thinker brings is normal so whatever size their question, our role is to hold our nerve. Try to avoid maximising comments like: *'We can't do that big thing justice'.* Keep rightsizing until you know the bit you need to explore. If the download is complex, remember that the thinker can only change how they do what they do in relation to others, so the only question in their gift to answer begins: *'How can I ...?'*

An alternative **SUBJECT:** *'What is our question?'*

This is a great way to get to the heart of the matter and is an example of building trust by using 'we' language for the work that we are doing here and now in this conversation. *'What is our question?'* is not asking the thinker *'What's your question for me?'* That would not be coaching. It would be advising.

TIME: *'In the (time) we have, which bit of that is it useful for us to focus on?'*

We are still rightsizing. As much as it is important to agree how long you have at the very start of the conversation, notice the difference when you ask the time question again after the subject:

Example: You: *'We have an hour – what would you like to think about?'*
Thinker: *'I want to think about relocating my department'.*
Becomes: You: *'What would you like to think about today?'*
Thinker: *'I want to think about relocating my department'.*
You: *'And in the hour we have, what is our question about that?'*
Thinker: *'How do I work with my colleagues who will have a longer commute and encourage them not to leave?'*

Stay optimistic. When you wait for the work to be the right size before you dive in, you will always have enough time for the work that needs to be done today.

I observe that the person with the perceived power controls the time. They don't mention it in the conversation much because they assume that it implies they are in a hurry. And if time is mentioned, it sounds like *'How long have we got?'* followed an hour later by *'We need to finish now. Let's continue the conversation next time'.*

Whether this is a formal conversation or a chat by the coffee machine, contracting for time is useful, and reduces the question to the right size for the time available.

OUTCOME: *'What would you like to be different by the end of this conversation?'*

This is future-focused and hopeful. Even when the thinker does not know what they would like to be different, you are setting an expectation together that, in some way, today's conversation will move them forward.

A question about outcome is never about a goal or what they would like to be different. It is to ensure that we are focusing on the things that are in their gift and that we can usefully explore together today in this conversation.

Example: Thinker: *'I'd like Thursday's meeting to go better'*.
You: *'And by the end of this conversation?'*
Thinker: *'I will have some ideas to enable them to move from being stuck'*.

KNOW: *'How will you know (today) that this conversation has been useful?'*

It is not your role to be a mind reader or to know how to make this conversation useful. Ask them. As soon as they have articulated how they will know – even if that is that they don't yet know – the work you do together will be easier, more effective and more in partnership.

Example: Me: *'How will you know this has been useful?'*
Thinker: *'I'll know it in my knower'*.

When a thinker said that to me, I had absolutely no idea what she meant. She was crystal clear. I did not need to know. Halfway through our conversation, I checked in:

Me: *'How's your knower?'*
Thinker: *'Half full'*.
Me: *'Is that enough?'*
Thinker: *'No'*.
Me: *'Are we heading for full or empty? And what do we need to do in the five minutes we have left to get there?'*

Please don't add the questions about knowers to your stash. Like many great questions they can't be used again. And they are an example of the value of the know question. It needs to be asked more than it needs to be answered and some people answer how they will know when asked about the outcome.

Example: *'I'd like to have three clear actions by the end of this conversation'*.
Sometimes the outcome and how they will know can be integrated into one question.
Becomes: You: *'What would you like to be different by the end of this conversation today that will mean that you know that Thursday's meeting is likely to go better?'*
Thinker: *'I will be more confident that I know what to do about X'*.

And they may not know how to answer the question. In that case, you are simply both clear that you don't know.

ROLE: *'How shall we do this work today?' (or what role would you like me to take?)*

It is normal in many conversations that the person who is perceived to have the power will lead how we work together. *'How shall we do this work today?'* implies partnership and gives permission to change how we work later in the conversation. The value of this clarity comes when you check in whether what you are doing together is useful, because this question made it clear that our way is not the only way. This question is particularly useful when you are having hybrid conversations and may need to change roles mid-conversation.

Every conversation happens only once. Being clear how to do the work together in this time and place is important. The thinker may know what will be most useful and be able to tell you. Or they have no idea and you can both move on. You have asked.

START: *'Where shall we start?'*

The thinker will know better than you do where to start the conversation. The content belongs to them. When you lead, you are most likely to go where you are most interested, excited or concerned. Starting where you left off last time may take them backwards. Asking where to start will enable the conversation to get to the heart of the matter earlier than normal. This is the question where thinkers go silent. They stop talking while they run through the situation, or question in their mind, noticing where is or is not a good place to start.

Example: Thinker: *'Let's start here'* … [silence] *'No, let's not'*.

In the internal dialogue that got this person there, they were already processing and gaining insights. The work was underway.

Sometimes the thinker will tell you precisely what question to ask them in response to *'Where shall we start?'* You could stay silent while you turn their excellent question into one of your own. And simply saying the equivalent of *'Go on then'* will allow their thinking to remain in flow.

While many conversations start at the beginning of a story, coaching is different. The beginning is rarely a good place to start. When they say *'I'll start at the beginning'*, ask whether that is useful to them. In coaching, you don't need to know anything unless it is useful for them to tell you because your role was never to solve their problem.

Provenance

In 2013, a course delegate said that he would find it useful to have a word to remember these opening questions. He came up with STOKeRS. The following week I wrote the questions on a flipchart and introduced the acronym. There was silence before one delegate called out that this was deep learning.

The stoker, he explained, is the person on the back of a tandem – a bicycle made for two people. Whatever our role – be it coach, clinician, minister, mentor or manager, this is our role. We are the stoker on the back of their bicycle giving balance and power at the start of a journey, and extra energy on hills. The thinker is the captain on the front of their tandem. It is their journey. When we are tempted to advise, lead, help or fix, we are doing the equivalent of jumping on the front of the tandem mid-ride. This serves neither the captain, the stoker, nor the journey. In fact, when a tandem stoker tries to interfere too much, both the stoker and the captain are at risk of injury.

The STOKeRS questions are designed to co-create the container. Make them your own. They are drawn from the ICF competency: establishing the coaching agreement.[6] They make coaching easier for you and more effective for the thinker. When Sarah Brisbane, an internal NHS coach, introduces this she says: '*If you have a problem with take-off, you are likely to have an uncomfortable flight*'.[7] Co-creating what we are doing in every conversation increases the potential for transformation. The purpose of the questions is simply to be clear together before we start doing any work:

- What are we doing today?
- How shall we do it?
- How will we know that we have done it?

Starting well enables the conversation to be more effective and easier to facilitate because we don't start doing the work until either we have a manageable question to explore or we have both agreed what we are here to do. That might be active engagement to unpick a question together or silently sitting together while the thinker recalibrates their thoughts and feelings.

Rightsizing the conversation sets the tone that we are here for a purpose. It means that we can get some useful things done in every session, including the first.

Pre-conversation

Not everyone arrives ready to do work. As much as we are together for a purpose, we are also two human beings having an encounter. Conversational encounters usually evolve as we follow common interests and make connections. When the start is unclear, we are less likely to be working in partnership because we haven't worked out what we are doing.

There are many reasons for unclear beginnings. One of you might think you have started the work, and the other is still in an arriving space. However great your listening and noticing superpowers, working out together what the work we are doing today is, while listening to the thinker downloading and decompressing complexity and emotion at the same time is complicated.

The coaching container rightsizes the work and increases potential for transformation. In the same way, in your mind it is useful to have a container

Figure 3 The pre-conversation

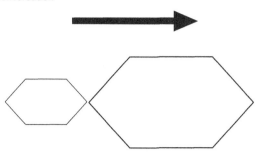

around the arriving. Let's call this a pre-conversation (Fig. 3). You don't need to explain this, but it reminds you to indicate more clearly verbally or physically when you are moving from the pre-conversation to the work.

> Example 1: The thinker arrives in the room, having just found out that their chain of restaurants has to shut because of Covid-19. They are in a high state of emotion. If you let this emotion run, your time could be hijacked by debriefing emotion. This may or may not be the most useful thing for them to do with you. You don't know. <Listening to what happened>
> Becomes: *'Would it be useful to take five minutes to let off steam and then we will work out what we need to do today?'*

The rest of the conversation might stay with the emotion. With a pre-conversation this is an intentional choice, not something you slip into. The thinker is in control of how to use the time.

> Example 2: They arrive ten minutes late saying they are overwhelmed with the number of balls they are juggling this week. <Listening to the overwhelm may grow it>
> Becomes: *'Is it useful to take ten minutes to get the balls out of your head and then we will work out what we need to do today?'*

I slipped a pad of blank paper and some pens over. The thinker started writing and circling a whole stack of words on the page. I could neither read nor understand it. *'That's better'*, they said as they came up for air. Holding the silence while they downloaded what was on their mind was more affirming and effective than talking about it. Getting them to tell me what was overwhelming them was only going to overwhelm them more. *'And what do we need to focus on today?'* allowed us to know what the work was we needed to do.

> Example 3: Greetings differ across cultures. And when we work with someone over time, we may be interested in their holidays, children or weekend, and may ask about these in service of building trust. Connecting is important but it risks switching into a conversation about both of us: *'Oh, I've been to Paphos – did you go*

snorkelling?' Without some kind of punctuation, it can be hard to move into a different kind of conversation.

Becomes: *'Shall we take five minutes to catch up on the summer and then we can work out what we need to do together today?'*

In some cultures, or contexts, it is inappropriate to begin the work together without greetings. Sometimes the pre-conversation takes longer than the work (Fig. 4). And the boundary in your mind means that when you get to the work you both become clear that is what you are doing.

Example 4: Catching up from last time is usefully done as a pre-conversation so that there is time and space to do some good work today. As much as it's great to find out if the coaching you did last time worked, checking in is not feedback or catching up for you. *'Tell me how the presentation went'.*

Becomes *'Is it useful to catch up? Why don't you take five minutes to say what was the learning from the presentation day, for you?'*

Example 5: A pre-conversation is useful when someone comes to the conversation and is unclear what they want to think about. Rather than you focusing on a theme, use the time for them to download. Notice the headlines and underbelly and offer them back: *'Would you like to download what's going on and then we will work out together what we need to do today?'*

Being clear together what is pre-conversation and what is the work means that:

- it has a time boundary and will not invade the whole conversation – unless it emerges that what the thinker is saying is the thing you need to explore together
- they know to give the five-minute version rather than the full story
- there is a boundary between looking back before you agree to look forward together
- you are not trying to two things at the same time – you can simply notice

And you are both clear when you are starting the work.

Figure 4 When arriving takes time

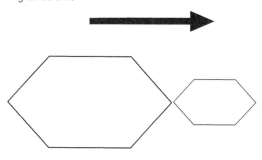

Figure 5 When the rightsizing does the work

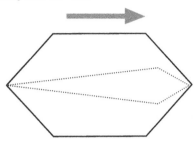

When they don't know

Not everyone who comes to a conversation is going to be clear about how they want to use the time. If they are clear what you are here to do, and you are staying with the rightsizing for your own clarity, it is not useful. Sometimes the rightsizing will take the whole conversation because it moves their thinking forward. As much as the container introduced in Fig. 1 is symmetrical, few conversations look like that in reality. Some are more like a carrot (Fig. 5). When this happens, finding the question provides enough clarity for them to be able to move forward without you.

Don't pick up where you left off

Unless we rightsize every conversation, we risk taking control and going to places that are no longer useful to the thinker. We can't expect to pick up where we left off.

Let's return to the metaphor of the plane. If a traveller is going from London to Brisbane, Australia, they don't need to be on a plane for the whole journey. We travel together for a while, and then we disembark and go our separate ways. Sometimes one journey together is enough. At other times we might travel together again. As much as there might be good reasons for establishing at the outset which bits of the journey we will travel together, we won't really know the answer to that until we set off.

Coaching is a journey where the expectation is that the thinker moves forward in some way. It is not about travelling the whole journey with them to their final destination. Although a contract for the coaching relationship clarifies where the thinker is heading and something about a useful way of working for us both, they will keep moving when we are not there. If they don't, we can talk about that together. If we metaphorically end our last meeting in Frankfurt en route to Australia, the next meeting will not begin at Frankfurt airport. By now they might be in Dubai and want our company as they explore how to get to Chile. Our task is to be with them for small parts of their journey. It is a fantasy that the coach has to travel the whole journey. That would be dependency.

We need to trust them to have the capacity to move forward. Our role is to do enough and not too much.

Applying beginnings at work

Rightsizing is not magic. You are not doing something to them. Give your colleague the STOKeRS questions on a card and invite them to use them to frame your conversation.

When you rightsize the question before you start doing the work, you will find that conversations and meetings are more useful.

Applying beginnings for experienced coaches

After your next coaching conversation, ask yourself how clear you both were about what you were doing before you started the work. When you both get lost, you share the responsibility to find your way through the conversation. Rightsize again: *'What's our question now?'*

Applying beginnings for coaching supervisors

How can you be even clearer about how you are working together in the supervision you offer?

Notes

1   International Coach Federation (ICF) (2019), *Updated ICF Core Competency Model*, October, available at: www.coachfederation.org/app/uploads/2019/11/ICFCompetencyModel_Oct2019.pdf (accessed 18 March 2020).
2   Topham, G. (2019), 'British Airways flight to Düsseldorf lands in Edinburgh by mistake', *The Guardian*, 25 March, available at: www.theguardian.com/business/2019/mar/25/british-airways-flight-dusseldorf-lands-edinburgh--mistake (accessed 27 March 2020).
3   International Coaching Federation (ICF) (2020), *ICF Core Competencies Rating Levels*, available at www.coachfederation.org/app/uploads/2017/12/ICFCompetenciesLevels Table.pdf (accessed 27 March 2020).
4   Einstein, A. (2012), *Are you solving the right problem?*, available at: www.hbr.org/2012/09/are-you-solving-the-right-problem (accessed on 27 March 2020).
5   Amabile, T. and Kramer, S. (2011), *The Progress Principle: Using Small Wins to Ignite Joy, Engagement, and Creativity at Work*, Cambridge, MA: Harvard Business Review Press.
6   International Coaching Federation (ICF) (2020), *ICF Core Competencies Rating Levels*, available at: www.coachfederation.org/app/uploads/2017/12/ICFCompetenciesLevels Table.pdf, (accessed 27 March 2020).
7   In conversation, with permission.

4 Simple questions

What the coaching bodies say

All three bodies quoted here agree that questions are about gaining new insights.

The EMCC notes that the coach '[r]esponds to the full sensory range of client communication, in the moment, to infer possible areas for questioning' and commends variety by being 'flexible in applying a wide range of questions to facilitate insight'.[1]

The Association for Coaching also speaks of 'ask[ing] powerful questions that move the client forwards towards the agreed outcome' as the coach 'asks questions to challenge [the] client's assumptions, elicit new insights, raise self-awareness and gain learning'.[2] And the ICF states that the coach 'facilitates client insight and learning by using tools and techniques such as powerful questioning, silence, metaphor or analogy ... asks questions about the client, such as their way of thinking, values, needs, wants and beliefs [and] asks questions that help the client explore beyond current thinking'.[3] The ICF goes on to mention silence, talking about a coach who 'creates or allows space for silence, pause or reflection'.

Face forward

The coaching bodies talk about 'maintaining forward momentum' (Association for Coaching) and that it is important to 'generate ideas about how they can move forward' (ICF). Tandem bicycles move forwards. Moving a bike backwards is tricky. Coaching is different from counselling and therapy because it is about the present and the future. Paying attention to some things in the past might be useful to the thinker and the general direction of travel still needs to be forwards. I have heard this described as 'so what, what next?' If it emerges that someone is unable or unwilling to move forward, it is a useful indicator that coaching is not what they need. Then you will be able to robustly work with them to think about what different kind of intervention might be useful.

Figure 6 Coaching is future-focused

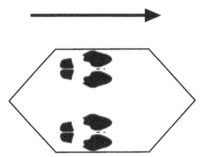

Figure 7 Forwards and backwards

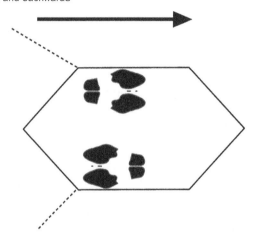

In most disciplines that use conversation, information is passed from one person to the other so that the person with the expertise, or indeed the perceived power, can cast an eye over it and offer affirmation, challenge or advice. Let's call that data transfer. It is often about the past. The more information that the thinker brings into the room, the more coaching risks looking like this and you end up doing the data processing. The purpose of a coaching style is that you facilitate their data processing.

Coaching is all about the future (Fig. 6). That means that we need to be facing forwards. Solution-focused coaching sprang from the therapeutic work of de Shazer and Berg.[4] I met a coach who was combining solution-focused coaching[5] with Whitmore's GROW model.[6] She asked me why she was struggling to facilitate forward movement in people coming for coaching. She told me: '*I use GROW to see the situation thoroughly – I can see whether they keep saying certain words*'. But our role is not to see the situation thoroughly, or to diagnose. It is for the thinker to see the situation thoroughly. If there is useful information for them in how they talk, it will emerge in other parts of the conversation.

Figure 8 What is your reality?

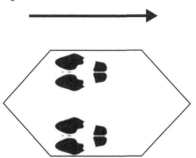

Co-creating the coaching container, described in Chapter 3, is about setting a clear boundary around the work you are doing together. All the STOKeRS questions are future-focused. This means that both coach and thinker are facing forwards as we begin the conversation. As soon as you ask about the past, or the thinker expresses a desire to fill you in on the detail, one or both of you has turned around (Fig. 7). You are now facing backwards (Fig. 8).

Asking a question about what is going on – or the story – is part of John Whitmore's GROW model,[7] which asks questions in four areas: What are your goals? What's the reality? What are your options? What will you do? When you invite the thinker to tell the story of their reality, both of you turn from facing the future and you are now facing backwards (Fig. 8). The more the thinker tells you, the more you are sending out the message: '*If I know that, maybe I can solve this for you*'. Moving from the language of problem-solving to exploring a question reduces the need to look back so much. If it is useful to the thinker to look back, changing the medium, described in Chapter 5, is one way of looking at the reality by standing back and noticing together. This is different from them telling you the story or giving you a case history.

If this conversation is to move their thinking forward, both coach and thinker need to get into new territory or look at old territory in a new way. If you are using a version of '*tell me your (back) story*' to build trust, try looking at it together: '*Tell yourself your back story and let's see what we notice*'. '*What have you tried already?*' is another question I hear coaches asking daily. It means that the thinker is using up their time reporting back to you. If that is going to be useful, bring it into the present: '*If you look at what you have tried already, what do you notice?*'

Unlike the future-focused container which you have made for the work you will do today, the past is unboundaried and very interesting. The more story the thinker tells you, the more they will explain. You are likely to become overwhelmed or seduced as you move away from the start of the container and into the past. If one of you recognises this and turns, you are now looking in opposite directions. In order for the thinker to start moving forward in this conversation, you both need to turn to face the future again. If one of you is still facing the past, you will get stuck. This is explained more simply in a video you can view at: https://youtu.be/QaHNuplokRM.

Occasionally, people do need to tell a story and listen to themselves in order to find themselves in it. You can tell that because you will see them thinking as they speak. A useful question to ask yourself is, *'who is being served by telling this story?'*

Interrupting

There is a difference in the pace when people are telling the story and when they are gaining new insights. The story that sounds like a reading from a book is more likely to be things they have spoken of many times before. In which case ask them: *'What will be different for you today if it's useful for you to tell this again?'* When transformation is occurring as the story new insights, you will hear it. It will be punctuated by pauses and 'um', and 'oh?'. Ask them. That's what partnership is about.

Given that coaching is different from other conversations, we need to demonstrate this in the way we work together from the outset. As children we were taught not to interrupt other people speaking. As adults, we don't hear much about not interrupting someone else's thinking. In conversations, we need to learn how to interrupt people's thinking less. This may mean that we interrupt their speaking more if they are telling us the story, and it is not giving them any insights. Interrupting in coaching is controversial. It is their space and interrupting can look directive. It is not directive – it is direct.

If you are not sure if what they are telling you is useful to them, ask them. That ensures partnership throughout the conversation. Check with questions like: *'Is this useful?'* or *'Is this giving you new insights?'* You may need to challenge.

Example:	*'Assume I know everything. What do we need to think about today?'*
Or:	*'I don't need to know that – unless it's useful for you to say it'.*

When a lot of information is downloaded into the conversation early, it is tempting to interrupt by going back to the beginning and revisiting the contract. That would be heading backwards. Try a future-focused interrupting question:

Example:	*'When we started we agreed we would be talking about xyz ...'.* (backwards)
Becomes:	*'And our question for today is?'*, *'What's your most important question about that for today?'* or *'And today?'*

Including the word 'today' in questions helps to be very clear that this is about what we are doing together here and now. When the download is all about other people, an interrupting and clarifying question to be clear what you are doing together today might be: '*And your question for today is – How can I …?*' Notice that you are offering them a sentence to complete, not to do the work yourself. Tone matters.

Whilst some people download a significant amount of narrative because they expect that is what you want to hear, some people just talk a lot without getting insight. Inviting them to do some thinking on the inside can be useful, when trust is strong enough. This is faster and can be more effective for them than speaking everything out loud. Although you might enjoy getting more information, you probably don't need to know what it is – because it may not be serving them.

Example: *'In your head, think about what's going on and what will be useful for us to think about together today …'.*

What are questions for?

Questions can bring transformation. If they are going to elicit new insights in someone else and enable them to move forward, how do we know what questions to ask? We bring a toolbox of questions and techniques from different parts of our life and work. These may come from recruitment and selection, appraisals, disciplinary, or from our experience as an expert in our field. In all those situations, we are likely to know what we want or need to know and therefore what questions to ask. In selection, the questions come from the paperwork – CVs and role descriptions. In education or safety, they may come from gaps in what is heard – or a desire to clarify. Coaching is different from other conversations, and it is useful to make that difference clear by the way in which we ask questions. Coaching questions need to enable the thinker to think. They are not about what you think you need to know, or indeed want to know.

About ten years ago, I wanted to write '*The Art of Powerful Questions*'. It was going to be full of the best coaching questions I had ever used or heard. I am glad that I didn't. Every day I hear about the pressure people trained in coaching feel to remember and ask the right questions. That pressure means that the conversation is between you, the thinker, the process, the pressure you are feeling and your resource book – or the parts of the book that you can remember mid-conversation. That is a lot of partners. There can be no master's degree in powerful questioning. A question is powerful not because of its eloquence but because of its capacity to enable the thinker to think. I don't mind travelling on a plane that is a little tatty and tired as long as it reaches the destination, and the flight is not too long. Great questions are about moving people forward. They can be tatty, too.

Every conversation we have is unique. Once you have begun the work of today's conversation, reusable questions might be valuable as a last resort. Not as a first choice.

Start with them

The best questions come from the thinker. They emerge from noticing

- what you hear
- what you see
- what you sense

and asking questions in service of enabling the thinker to do what is useful for them. If you want your conversations to be more effective and have a better outcome, start with the thinker. Notice well and say what you see with a question mark at the end. It takes less than a second to see or hear something and turn it into a question. There is no need to translate what you saw into a well-formed piece of English. The simplicity of the observation can get lost in translation. When a deep observation becomes a well-crafted and eloquent question, it can miss the point.

> Example: Thinker: [about a conversation to be had with a colleague]
> '*I want this ... I want that ... I am finding this difficult ...*'
> Coach: '*Who do you need to be for this conversation to be effective?*'
> Thinker: '*I don't know what you mean?*'

The coach had noticed that the thinker was using 'I' language and was focused on themselves. The observation was lost in translating what was seen into a question they knew had been useful before. The art of simplicity is to notice and say it. A more powerful question would have been: '*I want this ... I want that ... I am finding this difficult ...?*' And, only if necessary: '*And your colleague?*'

In most conversations, the distinction between observation (their stuff – what you saw) and opinion (your stuff – what you think) is unclear. It is useful for the thinker to know where questions are coming from. Then they can own their thoughts and not think that they are yours. Reflecting back 'I' language makes this distinction clear as long as you watch your tone. Notice the different impact:

> Example 1: '*You want this, you want that, you are finding this difficult?*' sounds like that could be your opinion or perspective.
> Example 2: '*I want this ... I want that ... I am finding this difficult ...?*' is clearly theirs.

Saying what you see is also useful if you seize the moment when the thinker does something in the room that they have been talking about at work.

> Example: The thinker was talking about the feedback they did not recognise about getting angry in meetings. As they spoke, their face was getting redder, and their volume louder. I said what I saw: '*Can I say what I see right now? I wonder if this happens in meetings?*'

People often demonstrate that they have an insight through words or a gesture and don't notice it. This is transformation. If they don't notice and we do, tell them. That gesture or a word can be the most powerful question of all:

> Example: I was observing someone talking about a big career choice. As he spoke, he held the options in both hands. When he talked about one, he looked at that hand, and when he talked about the other, he looked at the coach. Instead of forming a question about what they had seen, the coach simply held out their hands and repeated exactly his words and his gesture. 'So I could do this <LOOKS AT HER HAND> or I could do that <LOOKS AWAY>'. The thinker's first response was 'Did I do that?' And then he continued to explore what that might mean for him. The coach remained silent. The thinker became tearful in response to the quality of his new insights.

Commas, not full stops

Good thinking happens when there is flow. Minimal encouragers are words or gestures that the thinker will barely notice and which encourage flow. Think of them as punctuation. 'Uh huh', 'and?', 'mmm' and even a nod are like commas and encourage people to keep talking. When there is no sound or gesture, people do not feel heard.

'Coaching is more like golf than tennis', says Sarah Brisbane,[8] an internal NHS coach. Our role is not to catch the ball and throw back the next question. Our hope is that the question moves their thinking forward, and we walk together to where they are now. And if the question took us into the long grass, we can work out what to do next together. Whereas 'mmm' can encourage someone to continue to speak, 'okay' or its US equivalent 'got it' or 'gotcha' can sound like a full stop. It is as though you have caught the ball and the thinker is waiting for you to throw it back.

Minimal encouragers are impacted by your cultural context. When they sound like approval, they risk making the thinker try to please the coach.

Examples of neutral, minimal encouragers

So?
And?
Say more ...?
And now ...?
What else?
<Silence and a gesture>
Headlines – one or two words with a question mark

Short and simple

When I listen to conversations, I hear the coach take a breath as they catch what has been said, hold it, and turn it into a question. As the coach begins talking, the thinker is ready to respond but the coach completes the question. The thinker would have taken the first few words and made them their own. Now they are waiting politely for the coach to finish their sentences. A great question is simply enough to keep the thinker processing. Use your words wisely. The longer your questions, the more they will stop and listen to you and not to what is going on in them. Every word you speak is using a piece of the time you have together. You risk interrupting their thinking.

Your value does not come from how many words you use, or from the eloquence of your questions. The value you bring is to be fully present and enable another person to do what is needed to see things differently. When you are working in partnership, and the questions you ask are based on what you see or hear or sense, you only need to say as much as is necessary to facilitate new insights. The first three words may be enough to catalyse their thinking. They do not need to make sense anywhere else.

Tiny comments like 'And ...?' or 'So ...?' can create the sticky silence that enables the thinker to think new things. Too many words reduce the challenge. Less is more. And if you know you are a fixer, it is hard to offer unsolicited advice in a very short question.

A great question keeps thinking in flow or disrupts it in a productive way. It takes the thinker on a journey where they end in a different place from where they started. We need to encourage thinkers to reject questions that do not serve them well.

Show the working out

There are times when you cannot find the question, and three words will not be enough. Talking your way into a question in a stream of consciousness means that the thinker will follow you. This is confusing and will interrupt their thinking. They will try and interpret your intermediate ramblings and answer them. If you need to pause for a moment to find the question, and your search is in service of their thinking rather than your curiosity, then pause and show the working out. This indicates that the question is coming in a short while and that they don't need to answer the first part of what you are about to say:

Example: *'Let me think out loud. You have said <this> and <that> and I have observed <something> ... so my question is ...?'*

When you have a number of questions emerging that you could ask, rather than selecting the one you think is most useful, ask them. This demonstrates partnership.

Example: *'I'm asking myself questions about <this>, <that> and <the other> and am wondering whether any of those are useful for us today?'*

Great questions respect the container we have co-created for this conversation. If a question comes that is outside the contract for today, ask them.

Example: *'We were talking about practical job choices, and now we are talking about your lack of motivation – what's the most useful thing for us to do in the time we have?'*

Showing the working out respects the thinker's personal power in the conversation. This is fundamental to your partnership.

Don't need an answer

Not every question needs an answer. Asking it might be enough.

Example: *'Why are you staying in this job you describe as toxic?'*
Becomes: *'If I was going to be really challenging, I might be asking you what is keeping you in this job?'*

This second version brings the question into the room and gives the thinker the choice of answering or not. It is not a question I ask often. When I do it keeps them safe, but the question has still been asked.

In sync

When transformation is happening in a conversation, the thinker is likely to move ahead of you as they process internally. Everyone is different, so it is impossible to calculate how fast this happens. What we know is that people think significantly faster than they speak. This is especially true when the language of our dialogue is not their first language.

Great coaching happens when you and the thinker are working in sync. When you move too far ahead, you will leave them behind. If they leap you need to keep up; otherwise, you will be taking them backwards. Sensing pace is an inexact science, and sometimes you will get it wrong. Our role is to acknowledge when the thinker is either ahead of us, or in a parallel conversation and to ask them what we need to do next. *'Where are we now?'*, *'What do you know now that you didn't know before we started speaking?'* or *'Now you know that what do we need to do now?'* are more useful questions than *'What happened?'* *'What happened?'* is a backwards-facing question and only needs sharing if it is useful to the thinker. It respects their privacy because they don't need to tell you what it was.

The thinker may also not be in sync with themselves. Their body, mind and spirit may be moving at different speeds. Or they may be having a conversation with themselves at the same time as the one they are having with you. I had a seminal learning moment coaching someone who had rapid eye movement throughout the conversation. I asked: '*And the other conversation you are having?*' That happens quite often, and people are astonished that it is noticed. By noticing it, we invite the internal conversation into the room so that it begins to connect with the external even if they do not disclose what it was.

What does it look like to be in sync? Watching thousands of thinkers think, people speak with their body before they use words. This is about noticing position, pace and tone. Someone will say they are stuck and start to walk or move their feet. Simply notice and make the same gesture:

Example: Thinker: '*I can do it*', said slowly in a monotone
Coach: '*I can do it?*', said with a slight change of tone, '*Are you going to say that like you mean it?*'
Thinker: '*I CAN do it*', and they are back in sync.

Disposable

Most of our questions cannot be reused. Coach Yvette Elcock shared a conversation on LinkedIn where '*[the thinker's] logic was struggling to make sense of what she wanted to do next.* "*What would make your heart sing so loudly that your logic would rest a while?*"' asked Yvette, who described feeling the spark as the question unlocked something! Her question simply came from what was seen and heard and sensed in that moment.

Several people commented on LinkedIn that they loved the question so much they would add it to their collection. In conversation, Yvette told me: '*Yes those words worked at that moment in that context with me and my client, so simply importing the question into a different moment and different context could at best be clumsy and at worst unproductively disruptive*'.[9]

A question that is good in one conversation is not necessarily useful in another and needs to be discarded. The refuse sack or golden bin bag is an essential tool for every coach. It is a place to lose the question you formed a few minutes ago as your companion has continued to explore beyond. It was excellent. And has lost its usefulness.

Much of what we ask is not useful. Asking questions is an inexact science like theatre improv where you make an offer and the other person may or may not take it up. When you ask, notice how the question lands and notice whether it is evoking new thinking or taking the thinker back to what they know already. If it's going backwards, let them dispose of it.

Only a few standard questions are useful: rightsizing questions to create the coaching container and those that move learning forward. These are usually about what we are doing together here and now in the conversation.

Figure 9 The beginning, the middle and the end

WHAT? SO WHAT? NOW WHAT?

Process questions

Many books and papers have been written about different types of questions. I think that there are two types:

1 there and then questions
2 here and now questions

There and then questions are about the situation or the stuff that the thinker brings – the story – past, present and future. Here and now questions are about the person who is here and what we are doing together, today, in this conversation.

People answer the questions that we ask them, so when we are asking questions about content or story (there and then) there is a risk that we get stuck there with them. Content questions have value occasionally – as long as we remember that we are neither analysts nor investigators. We are thinking partners as someone else processes at a depth that serves them.

In *Making Questions Work*,[10] Dorothy Strachan talks about three phases of a conversation which can usefully overlay the coaching container (Fig. 9). Strachan's 'What?' is the beginning phase as we open up the container. The exploring phase, where much of the work is done, is 'So what?'. The ending phase, as the conversation is ended in partnership, is 'Now what?'. All three of her questions are about the process – the here and now – and are at the heart of the partnership that we co-create. They have nothing in them from the content or the story. Process questions keep the thinker thinking.

Process questions as you co-create the coaching container

SUBJECT: *'What is your question for today?'*
TIME: *'In the (amount of time) we have, which bit of that is it useful to focus on?'*
OUTCOME: *'What would you like to be different by the end of this conversation?'*
KNOW: *'How will you know (today) that this conversation has been useful?'*
ROLE: *'How shall we do this work today?'*
START: *'Where shall we start?'*

Apart from '*Where shall we start?*', all the rightsizing questions can be asked at any stage of the conversation, and as many times as is useful as long as they are for the thinker to gain clarity and not for you. If you are feeling unclear, ask them: '*Are we clear enough?*'
Don't start doing the work until you are clear together:

• What are we doing today?
• How are we going to do it?
• How will we know we have done it?

Poohsticks is a quintessentially English game described in A.A. Milne's children's classic *The House at Pooh Corner*.[11] Sticks, or grass, are dropped into a stream on one side of a bridge, and the players run to the other side to see which comes out first. When you play this game by the side of any stream or river, some sticks will invariably get stuck in weeds or tree roots alongside the water. Some players stand back and watch their stick float downstream. They may hold a longer stick or branch, and tap the stick only when it gets caught by weeds. Others will tap and poke all the way, which results in the stick sinking and the player losing the game. Enabling the stick to find the flow of the stream means it can naturally find its own way. The purpose of the middle part of the coaching container is to do only enough to keep the flow to enable the thinker to explore, process and gain new insights. Our role is to enable them to do this, not necessarily to use words.

Process questions at the end

• '*And now?*'
• '*What next?*'
• '*Who else?*'
• '*When?*'

My favourite ending question emerged from someone on a course in Luton. She was a social worker and concerned that by creating a container for the conversation, much of what the thinker arrived with at the beginning of the conversation is not dealt with. Just because the thinker needs to continue to process does not mean that they need to do that with you – unless they decide that is the best way forward for them.

Example   '*There is a lot left unexplored. Why don't you bring that to our next conversation?*'

can create dependency. What matters is that we acknowledge it and ensure that they know what the next step is in their thinking. Her question was three words: '*And the rest?*'

This normalises the work left undone and demonstrates that we believe that the thinker is able to take the next step. These are closed questions because they enable us to land the conversation.

We process you for action

While many disciplines use 'you' in questions such as '*Where are you in your thinking now?*', using 'we' for our work in the here and now keeps us in closer company. I use questions like '*Where are we now?*' and '*What do we need to do next?*', which are effective in the conversation as long as you keep the action questions about them: '*What is your next step?*'

Getting lost

A conversation that you might have on a subject with someone now will look totally different in an hour's time, in a different place or with a different coach. And one or both of you will get lost from time to time. This is normal. It is neither about a lack of skill from you nor stuckness in them. No formula will stop you from getting lost.

When you co-create the container together, you are demonstrating partnership right from the very beginning. Checking in on the process is the only way to ensure that you continue to partner throughout. And it is completely normal to share responsibility when you are getting lost. This checking in is called re-contracting. It is about rightsizing again.

> Examples: '*Where are we now?*'
> '*Is this useful?*'
> '*What do you know now that you didn't know when we started?*'
> '*What insights have you had?*'
> '*What do we need to do in the rest of our time today to get where you need to be?*'
> '*What's your most important question, now?*'

The wrong question

You are a human being. Some of your questions will not serve the work you have agreed to do together. If you are halfway through talking and you know that what you are saying is not useful, invite them to ignore it, take a breath and ask a simpler question. In the pause, they might find the right question. As much as this might feel strange, the alternative is that you complete the question that you know is not useful, and then you sit and listen to them responding to it. Don't apologise, drop it, pause and move on. If you apologise, the focus of the conversation shifts from them to you. And this is not about you. This requires bravery. When you lose confidence because you have asked a substandard question, they will lose confidence. Trust the process and trust the partnership that you will find a way through. I remember early on in my coaching career asking a question. The other person replied: *'That's the wrong question'*. I think my silence was frozen. In the pause he said, *'But the right question is …'*. A long time passed while he answered his question.

Don't contain the answer

If the answer is in the question, it is not a question. It is a solution in disguise. Roger Schwarz, author of *The Skilled Facilitator,*[12] was heard to say that if you can add 'you idiot' to the end of a question without significantly changing the meaning, then it is not a question. For example, *'Have you talked to your line manager, (you idiot?)'*. This is a useful habit to lose in other conversations, too.

Offering an answer without permission demonstrates that we believe that the thinker is unable to come up with an idea of their own. *'Have you tried this?'* implies *'because I think you have not'*. That is not partnership. Sometimes input is useful. How and when to put that in is covered in Chapter 5.

Don't talk to the wavy people

Coaching is different from other conversations. It is about enabling the thinker to think. It is not about interrogating the problem, which distracts from the task in hand – which is the two of you engaged in conversation about their question. They come to think about how they engage with other people and/or things. Imagine that you are coaching someone who is exploring how to get buy-in from their team, and particularly how they can manage an older colleague who has been in the organisation a long time and is not engaging with the changes that are emerging.

> Example: *'Tell me a bit about your colleague and your team'*. You are interrogating the problem. Instead of talking to the thinker here and now, you are now talking to their colleagues there and then.
> *'What have you tried already?'* They know that.

If you have experienced (or are experiencing) something similar in your own context, you are now distracted by their colleagues and your own. You are listening through the filter of your own stuff. Their voice is being drowned out as you listen to your distractions and talk to theirs.

You have brought competing voices and complexity into the room. This is like having other people dancing around the conversation. Don't talk to the

Figure 10 Don't talk to the wavy people

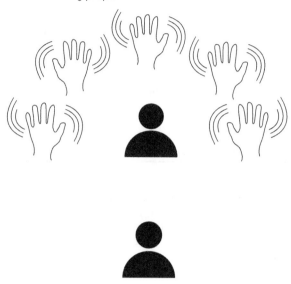

wavy people (Fig. 10). This is demonstrated in a video you can watch at https://youtu.be/fjKaKuHznqs.

Talk to the person here and now and not to their problem. The only thing in your gift in this conversation today is the encounter that you are having together at this moment. That's what will enable the thinker to feel heard. The only thing in their gift is their own behaviour, values, thoughts and attitudes and how they manage those in relation to the people with whom they have contact. Many hours are spent in organisations talking to or about wavy people. '*Right here, right now, what do we need to do?*' brings the attention right back to what Hawkins calls '*the space between us*'.[13] It is a quick way of losing the wavy people and returning to refocus on what we are doing together today.

> Examples: '*What do we need to do here so that you can do that there?*'
> '*And your question for today is – How can I …?*'

It may be that it is useful to look at the stuff together. That needs to be done in partnership, which looks different from you asking questions about it. Changing the medium (Chapter 5) is a way of doing that.

Intuition

Questions come from what we see and hear and from what we sense. Some people name that sensing intuition. If you want to explore where it comes from, neuroscience gives plenty of insight into intuition.[14] Our question is about what we do with it.

If you are intuitive, in a conversation you might have an intuitive insight, make a hypothesis and begin to ask questions to see whether or not you are right. Now you are working in service of your hypothesis. This risks leading the thinker into a place that is interesting to you and which may or may not be useful to them. Managing well what you sense is all about timing and discernment. Psychotherapist Nigel Wellings says that '*leaving ourselves on one side, and yet bringing ourselves into the room as and when appropriate is an art we learn from experience: Never know better, never know first, and to know when we think we know*'.[15] Intuition is useful in coaching. And knowing better and knowing first are not partnership.

Notice intuition and tread lightly. This is an inexact science, and sometimes we will get it wrong. Climber Alex Honnold eloquently said: '*There's a constant tension in climbing, and really all exploration, between pushing yourself into the unknown but trying not to push too far. The best any of us can do is to tread that line carefully*'.[16] That tension is true in coaching. A useful question to ask yourself is: '*How do I share the intuition without becoming the meaning-maker?*'

> Examples: *'I'm wondering ...?'*
> *'The word "..." has come into my mind?'*

Are not for you

Managers put the word 'me' into sentences to soften them. Conversations in the workplace begin with questions like '*Tell me what's going on*'. This has two functions. First, people feel heard when they tell you things. Second, it gives the facilitator of the conversation the data they need to be able to offer insights, advice and solutions. In selection, '*Can you tell me more about that?*' means that the candidate has not given you all the information you would like.

Coaching is different. Although 'me' softens, in coaching it subtly moves the responsibility so that instead of you exploring together, the thinker is telling you things. Coaching questions need to give insight to the thinker, not to you. '*You are not here to verify, instruct yourself, or inform curiosity or carry report*' wrote T.S. Eliot.[17] The thinker needs to be seeing things in a different way. You do not need to know or understand more about their situation. Keep 'me' out of your questions. If the invitation to expand and explore is because it will be useful to them, then ask the question differently: '*Say more ...?*'

> Example: *'Clarify for me'.*
> Becomes: *'Are you clear enough?'*

Always ask permission. This moves '*Let's explore that*', which is leading, to '*Shall we explore that?*', which is partnership with permission. I learned that one from meeting a number of people who have felt brutalised by coaches whose work has made them feel done to.

Great questions last

When questions are great, they keep the thinker processing. This means that they will not need to be followed too quickly by another question. Don't minimise the insight or the impact by keeping talking. If it is a great question, let it sit. It is well equipped to do what needs to be done without you following close behind.

I am reminded of Peter Levine's definition of trauma, '*too much, too fast, too soon*',[18] when I hear a series of questions being asked in quick succession. Too many questions too quickly are overwhelming. Ask one and wait. You will not need to form the next question until this one has done its work or been discarded.

Why not why?

Asking why can be received as a request to explain, justify or hypothesise about what someone else might be thinking or planning. A friend got stuck in an interview when they asked the thinker why he wanted the job – and he couldn't answer! Often, we cannot answer the question 'why?'. In selection, a question like '*What are the reasons you have applied for this job?*' allows candidates to answer more easily. The same is true in coaching.

Coaching is about moving forward. 'Why?' is a backwards-facing question, so turning it around can be more useful:

Example   '*Why did you do that?*'
Becomes   '*You're doing that because ...?*'

Although it might be useful to ask questions that glance backwards, interrogating the past is unproductive unless you are taking a step back and exploring the situation together.

Example: '*Why do you think they did that?*' is hypothesis and you are enquiring.
Becomes: '*If we stand in their shoes, what do we notice?*' asks the same question from a different place.

'Why?' is useful when it is digging down to explore purpose. Simon Sinek's *Start with Why*[19] is a useful resource for this.

Silence

When the coach leaves space, transformation is more likely to happen. Moons observed that the coach needs to stay silent, as '*an insight is characterised by a moment of silence, a moment in which clients seem to withdraw within themselves. During these moments of silence, the brain is not thinking logically or analytically, but engaging a part of itself that makes links across the whole brain'.*[20]

A coach I supervise arrived with a piece of paper that he takes to work. On it is written 'WAIT: Why Am I Talking?' This a great tool to have in front of you in a coaching conversation or a meeting. Let asking a question be your second option after saying nothing. *'Don't talk unless you can improve the silence'* said poet Jorge Luis Borges.[21] When you observe people using silence well, it is not the anxious emptiness where neither party knows what to say – but a sticky silence that allows the thinker to continue to think.

Whilst demonstrating coaching to a group there was a silence that lasted more than two minutes. One of the group expressed extreme discomfort, describing the silence as intolerable. He wanted me to break it. In the debrief, the thinker asked: *'What silence?'* When you agree with yourself, or with the thinker, that only they will break the silence, you will begin to learn to use silence well. When you let them break the silence, it will be of a length that is useful to them. Learn to watch their body language and their eyes or the side of their face to see whether they are thinking. If they are thinking, leave them. That is an important part of the coaching process. When they are ready, they will look at you. Nancy Kline, when having a conversation, asks people to indicate when they have done all their thinking lest she interrupts their silence before they are ready to move on.[22]

Words are overrated. Great coaching is not about how much you say – it is about whether what insights and knowing the thinker has had after the conversation, or indeed the whole coaching process is over. In an interview with BBC Hardtalk, actor Alan Rickman said: *'You only speak because you wish to respond to something you've heard … What you have to say is completely incidental'.*[23]

It never ceases to amaze me the capacity people have to think and understand and find ways forward. Silence can be the most powerful question of all. If you know that your questions interrupt or assume or get in the way of other people's thinking processes, try saying nothing and keeping out of the way.

Who leads?

Coaching is different from other conversations because the container does the work and carries some of the process. It is not only dependent on the quality of our questions (Fig. 11). The ICF describes this by saying *'the coach trusts that value is inherent in the process versus having any need to create value'.*[24]

You are in this together. And there is no one right way to have a conversation. Indeed, if you had the same conversation at a different time or in a different place, it would look different. Exploring will take you both to new and unknown places. There will be times when neither of you knows where you are going. This is their journey. As much as you will notice along the

Figure 11 The container does the work

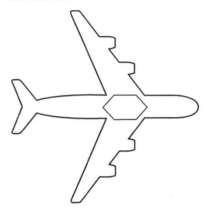

way, the thinker needs to lead while you follow close behind. When you get too far ahead, they are likely to follow you regardless of whether it is useful to them.

If you would like to experience this, coach and walk if you are both able to. Before you set off, invite the thinker to pick the route as you go. This is to avoid the awkward moment when you get to a junction and remember that you do not know who is leading. All you need to do is walk alongside and about an inch behind them. This is the best way to learn to let them lead, to pace, and to learn how to use silence because they are in control. When, or if, they want you to speak, they will turn to look at you. In this position, one inch behind, you will also see the side of their face and notice whether they have new insights.

We don't know what questions will move someone else's thinking forward. We don't know what they already know. As much as we are experienced in having conversations, this conversation is unique. This human being, their question, this time and this place will never exist again. You might think that you know where this conversation might go, and you have no idea what has happened in the interim since you last spoke.

As you start a conversation, you may feel under pressure to ask some great questions. You try one, and it doesn't work. So you try another. And if the thinker doesn't seem to be gaining any new insights, you will start working harder. This is leading. The harder you work, the less hard they will work. For a demonstration of this, watch the video at https://youtu.be/sR8QbAhX-os.

When you rightsize the question at the outset, the thinker starts to lead. And when you come to a fork in the conversation, ask them which way you should travel together. Re-contracting questions like '*Where are we?*' and '*What do we need to do next?*' keep them in the lead and keep the work in partnership. If they choose one fork and you had a great question for a different one, you can offer that at the end for them to take away. You can't explore everything. They are the best expert in their own lives.

Great questions don't need to have an answer

I took to coaching the question: '*What is making me sabotage my days off?*'. The outcome of my exploration was not an answer. It is a new question that sat with me for months and then became even more a gift in a new world of lockdown and social distancing. Every time I have a day off, I ask myself: '*What do I need to do today that is lifegiving for me?*' The new question has changed everything. Great questions do not need to have an answer.

In *Letters to a Young Poet*, Rainer Maria Rilke talks about the value of wondering over problem-solving: '*Do not now seek the answers, which cannot be given you because you would not be able to live them. And the point is, to live everything. Live the questions now. Perhaps you will then gradually, without noticing it, live along some distant day into the answer*'.[25]

Given the uncertainty of the world as we know it, knowing some of the questions and living with them can, in the end, produce a much more fruitful outcome than rushing straight for an answer. Not every question we ask needs an answer. We need to be brave and tolerate the thinker's not knowing. That enables them to be more brave, too.

One at a time

Asking one question at a time makes them more effective – even if you think that the first version was inadequate, leave it and see if it works. Avoid stacking questions.

Equally, if you need to do two things together in a conversation and one is not coaching, have one conversation at a time. I learned this when I listened to a coach trying to do coaching while the thinker wanted to give positive feedback on the effectiveness of the coaching to date. Having one conversation at a time is also useful if the thinker discloses a risk to themselves, to others or by others. That conversation is best navigated when it is clear the coaching part of the conversation has finished. Clear boundaries are empowering.

Ask questions from a different place

In Chapter 5, we explore asking questions from a different physical space. You can also ask questions from a different part of the person. If you use the premise that people are body, mind and spirit, you can ask a question from a different place if they are stuck in one mode.

> Example: '*This happened, that happened, something else happened*' – this is mind or facts.
> '*How does that feel?*' – a body or emotion question.

Another place is to ask questions that are mismatched. For example, when they are using a lot of words, asking a one-word question comes from a different place.

Enough is enough

People often have very specific goals: '*I want a job that gives me satisfaction*', '*I want to do a piece of work that's good*', '*I want to make a decision that feels safe*'. Somewhere in there is an assumption that this goal needs to be very satisfying or good or safe, and often that stops people from starting. Try changing the question: '*What's satisfying enough?*', '*What's safe enough?*', '*What's good enough?*' Using the word 'enough' can rightsize the distance to the goal.

Not choosing is a choice

It's easy for people to get stuck feeling that they have no choices. We all have choices. When someone feels stuck, they can choose to do nothing. That is a legitimate choice.

Recently I have been struck that we may know what our choices are and still hold back from exercising them. If that's happening to someone, a useful question can be: '*Do you know how you will choose how to choose? Or when to choose?*'

When questions are not safe

Everything I have written so far about questions assumes that you are in a culture where questions are safe and an acceptable way of engaging in conversation. What happens when questions are not safe?

Jennifer Giezendanner has extensive experience of working in Africa and Asia. In a blog post for Global Learning Partners,[26] she describes her experience of trying to ask powerful questions in a society where questions can be used by someone with more institutional or cultural power to humiliate a subordinate. In conversation with a cross-cultural organisation where I am working, we recently described this as places with a fixed power differential. Question marks don't work in every culture.

'*So*', writes Giezendanner, '*I tried an experiment. Instead of asking the question as a question, I rephrased it as a gentle command, like this:*

> *Example 1:* "What dreams do your village people have for their futures?"
> *[Becomes]:* "Tell me about the dreams your village people have for their futures".

Example 2: *"Why are some families more successful in raising their children than others?"*

[Becomes]: *"Tell me about what families do who raise their children successfully"'*.

She found that a slight change of emphasis moved from a test for the correct answer to give people the confidence to have insights and share them. Another useful phrase she used is *'In your opinion, tell me ...'*.

Over time, as trust builds, people can learn to engage with open questions. In some cultures, this trust-building will take time. Go slowly and notice resonance between people's words, eyes and body language. If they are out of sync, you may need to slow down.

A note about powerful questions

Start with the resource which is the individual who is with you. Use your book of powerful questions as your very last resort.

Applying great questions at work

Whether or not you are coaching, the best way to improve the quality of your questions is to record a one-to-one encounter and listen back. Notice what a question was for. Now notice whether it did what it set out to do.

Applying great questions for experienced coaches

If you would like to know how effective your questions are, try recording a conversation, with permission. That is the only way to access the real data that will enable you to be even more useful in conversations. Unless there are commercial reasons not to, many thinkers recognise that this is useful development for you. In fact, they might ask for the recording so that they can remember what you explored together. Recordings should be deleted after you have listened to them or shared them with your supervisor or mentor.

Listen to the thinker:

- Notice where your questions came from – was it from what they said?
- Notice the impact of the question – pace and timing.
- Are you both going in the same direction?
- Are you looking forwards or backwards?
- What assumptions have you made?

If you would like to work on the pace of your questions, find someone who will partner with you as you grow:

- Coach as you walk and talk – learn only to ask when they look at you.
- If you are sitting, use a talking stick. After the rightsizing, they hold the stick. You only ask a question when they give it to you.

If you know that you talk too much, contract with the thinker at the beginning of a conversation that you won't break the silence – it's up to them to tell you when they are ready to speak again.

Access recordings of other people coaching or go to places where you can do that. Instead of watching the process, simply watch the thinker think.

- What are you noticing when you are not forming questions?
- Notice how much is your input and how much is their processing.

Applying great questions for coaching supervisors

Observing real conversations with the people you supervise will enable you to stand back together and notice where the learning is about asking questions. Even when they are unable to record client sessions for commercial reasons, they will be able to record something.

Notes

1 European Mentoring and Coaching Council (EMCC) (2015), *EMCC Competence Framework V2*, September, available at: https://emccuk.org/Public/Professional_ Development/Competence_Framework/Public/1Resources/Competence_Frame-work.aspx?hkey=ad98bd86-8bb8-4435-913d-5258f6774375 (accessed 19 March 2020).
2 Association for Coaching (2012), *AC Coaching Competency Framework*, revised June 2012, available at: https://cdn.ymaws.com/www.associationforcoaching.com/ resource/resmgr/accreditation/rclac/supporting_documenation/coaching_compe-tency_framewor.pdf (accessed 27 March 2020).
3 International Coaching Federation (ICF) (2019), *Updated ICF Core Competency Model*, October, available at: https://coachfederation.org/app/uploads/2019/11/ICF-CompetencyModel_Oct2019.pdf (accessed 18 March 2020).
4 De Shazer, S. (1994), *Words Were Originally Magic*, New York: W.W. Norton.
5 Jackson, P. and McKergow, M. (2006), *The Solutions Focus: Making Coaching and Change Simple*, London: Nicholas Brealey.
6 Whitmore, J. (2002), *Coaching for Performance: GROWing People, Performance and Purpose*, London: Nicholas Brealey.
7 Ibid.
8 In conversation, with permission.
9 In conversation, with permission.
10 Strachan, D. (2006), *Making Questions Work: A Guide to How and What to Ask for Facilitators, Consultants, Managers, Coaches, and Educators*, San Francisco, CA: Jossey-Bass.
11 Milne, A.A. (2011), *The House at Pooh Corner*, London: Egmont Children's Books.

12 Schwarz, R. (2002), *The Skilled Facilitator: A Comprehensive Resource for Consultants, Facilitators, Coaches, and Trainers*, 2nd edition, New York: Wiley.

13 Hawkins, P. and Turner, E. (2019), *Systemic Coaching: Delivering Value Beyond the Individual*, Abingdon: Routledge.

14 Gladwell, M. (2006), *Blink: The Power of Thinking Without Thinking*, London: Penguin.

15 Wellings, N. and Wilde McCormick, E. (2000), *Transpersonal Psychotherapy*, London: Sage.

16 Honnold, A. (2015), 'Climber Alex Honnold: What risk means after Dean Potter', *Time Magazine*, 28 May, available at: https://time.com/3898371/alex-honnold-dean-potter-climbing/ (accessed 1 April 2020).

17 Eliot, T.S. (1943), *Four Quartets*, New York: Harcourt, Brace.

18 Heard by Lynn Stoney at conference on Global Trauma in Zurich.

19 Sinek, S. (2011), *Start with Why: How Great Leaders Inspire Everyone to Take Action*, London: Penguin.

20 Ibid.

21 Attributed to Jorge Luis Borges.

22 Kline, N. (1999), *Time to Think: Listening to Ignite the Human Mind*, London: Ward Locke.

23 BBC Hardtalk (2010), Interview with Tim Sebastian and Alan Rickman, BBC, available at: https://www.youtube.com/watch?v=BfytKK6gyVE (accessed 1 April 2020).

24 International Coaching Federation (ICF) (2020), *ICF Core Competencies Rating Levels*, available at: www.coachfederation.org/app/uploads/2017/12/ICFCompetenciesLevels Table.pdf (accessed 27 March 2020).

25 Rilke, M. (1993), *Letters to a Young Poet*, trans. M. Norton, New York: W.W. Norton.

26 Giezendanner, J. (2015), *What to do when questions are not safe*, available at: www.globallearningpartners.com/blog/what-to-do-when-questions-are-not-safe/ (accessed 27 March 2020).

5 Simple exploring

What the coaching bodies say

The middle of the conversation is about exploring. The Association for Coaching states that the coach: *'helps broaden a client's perception of an issue and challenges to stimulate new possibilities; supports ... to generate options to achieve agreed outcomes, provides observational feedback where relevant, leaving the client free to choose to act upon it or not ... offering "here and now" feedback'.*[1] The EMCC says: *'Uses a range of techniques to raise awareness, encourage exploration and deepen insight ... enables significant and fundamental shifts in thinking and behaviour ... adapts approach/technique in the moment in response to client information, while also holding a focus on outcomes.*[2] The EMCC also promotes using *'tools and techniques to help the client work towards outcomes'.* The ICF also talks about *'facilitat[ing] client insight and learning by using tools and techniques'.* Their tools come from the thinker *'such as powerful questioning, silence, metaphor or analogy'*, asking *'questions that help the client explore beyond current thinking'.*[3]

The middle of the conversation is usually where most of the work gets done and where new insights begin to emerge (Fig. 12). How long it is depends on how clear the thinker was when they arrived, and whether the rightsizing has already done a significant amount of the work. In the CLEAR model, Hawkins

Figure 12 Exploring

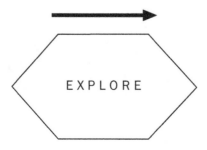

and Smith[4] call this stage 'exploring'. Transformation is more likely to happen when:

- you rightsized what you were doing today at the start of the conversation – even when the clarity is that you don't know what that is
- the exploring is done by and is in service of the thinker
- the conversation is focused on the present and the future
- the thinker makes their own meaning
- you agree together to change the contract if the real thing you need to be working on is different from what you first agreed

Mid-flight

While most of the work happens in the take-off and landing, most of the miles on a plane journey are covered mid-flight. As a passenger, we trust that the pilot is doing their job, even when we cannot see or hear them. It is only when they are needed that they say anything at all. Like a plane journey, coaching is about giving the process and the person our full attention. While the process and the thinker are doing the work, you can be silent and only need to ask questions where necessary.

A change of perspective is useful to track the journey of a plane using radar or a map. This is also true of the conversation. Getting too involved in the thinker's story and in their stuff risks you getting lost with them. The skill of navigating the middle of the conversation is to support the thinker to look differently, and for you to hold your nerve that you will find a way through together. I call this being attentively not bothered. There is an English saying that you can't see the wood for the trees. This means that you are so focused on each individual tree or the small details, that you lose sight of the whole. There is an art to giving your full attention and keeping away from the detail enough to maintain that different perspective.

Who is the exploring for?

This middle part of the conversation is a place for the thinker to explore and get a new perspective. Although your preference may be to ask questions to understand and to gather data, a coaching style is different from other conversations. It is not about your understanding, or gaining enough information to be able to offer advice or a solution.

Forensic pathology is my favourite genre of writing. I love the thrill of following the pathologist as they piece things together. They do the work. They make the connections. I don't think that the curiosity of a forensic pathologist serves the thinker. Forensics are the domain of subject experts. A coaching style is not about being a subject expert. It is about enabling someone to be curious about their own stuff. They need to make their own meaning. Your role is to be with them, notice together and most significantly to enable them to notice for themselves. If you are truly working in partnership, you can't think that you have solved the puzzle first and use the conversation to check out your hypothesis. We live in an unpredictable world. What people bring to conversations is more a mystery than a puzzle. Your skill is to learn to tolerate the tension of not knowing everything. It is not easy. And it takes bravery. If you are doing most of the work, why would they? Coaching is about partnership, not about turning someone into a passive receiver.

Every individual is different. Whether this is your first or your thousandth one-to-one, you don't know how to have this conversation with this person in this moment. You need to co-create what and how you are doing today. If that is unclear to them, keep rightsizing. And remember that having no idea what you are doing together is also a contract – as long as that is what you have both agreed.

Show the working out

As much as my fantasy was to be a forensic pathologist, my first job was as a maths teacher. I used to encourage my students to show the 'working out' when they were doing calculations. Unless they did that, it was impossible to give any useful insights to support their learning. In coaching, it is great when the thinker makes leaps forward. It is their conversation. But when you leap, you lead. Simply and in as few as words as possible, share what you have noticed that got you to that question or observation.

We use a version of this in our team, and it can be useful in mentoring, too. When a colleague says to me *'How much shall I charge for this?'*, I respond: *'Shall I tell you what I'm thinking?'* Instead of giving them the answer, they are getting insights into some of the factors that I think about to make a good decision in this area. Next time, they will be more able to make a good, well-informed decision of their own.

This is partnership. The working out is what you are thinking about what you might do now. It is not telling them how anxious you are. You will learn to manage that better over time as your trust in the process increases.

You *will* get lost

People starting out using a coaching style worry that they don't know what they are doing. This anxiety reduces your capacity to notice and to be fully present. For me, one of the signs of mastery is that you are comfortable not knowing what you are doing. We will work out how to have this conversation together – all the way through from the beginning to the end.

There will be times when you get lost and do not know what to do. You will always have moments where you miss things. You will ask questions that are not useful and may be distracting. This is normal. Noticing how your interventions land with the thinker will enable you to know when to check in.

In other conversations, when you are perceived to have power, you will make decisions about which way to go every time there is a lull or a fork in the conversation. You make hundreds of micro-decisions. Being lost is not a failure on your part. This is normal. Hold your nerve. Simply ask them every time you come to a fork in the road, '*What do we do next? Is this working? What do I need to do differently?*' This is widely known as re-contracting. It requires bravery. And it makes coaching easier.

Don't apologise

If you are working together in service of the thinker having new insights, some of what you do or say will not serve the conversation at all. Even the most experienced coaches sometimes ask terrible questions. The skill comes in what you do next. However great a coach you are, you are not a magician. Move on and don't apologise. If you apologise, both of you are turning backwards. That will interrupt the thinker's thinking. Keep looking ahead.

> Example: '*Shall we stand and look at that from a different place?*' You stand, the thinker looks confused, and the next question results in a blank stare: '*I'm sorry, I thought that might be useful, and it clearly was not …*'

The apology puts the focus on you. Moving on you could say: '*What would be useful right now?*'

Of course, there is sometimes an ethical aspect to an apology. Here I am talking about asking the wrong question. If you have broken an ethical code, then, of course, an apology will be needed.

Re-contracting

It is a long way from the beginning of a conversation to the end. Given that you are not a mind reader, you will not know if the work you are doing together is useful. This means that once you have started you will need to check in regularly that the conversation is serving the thinker and that they are getting new insights. Re-contracting is about the process. It is not about your performance, so be clear that your checking in questions are about the work and not about how well you are doing. Start early and check in regularly. Is the way you are working together useful? Is it moving them forward and bringing new insights?

Re-contracting is more natural when you began by asking the role (R) question in STOKeRS: *'How shall we do this?'* Even if the thinker barely understood the question when you asked it, you were demonstrating that this conversation is being co-created. To be full partnership, that co-working needs to modelled all the way through every conversation. Re-contracting questions are about the process – what you are doing together in the room, and about insights – what they are learning.

Process checking questions include:

- *'Where are we now?'* and
- *'Is this useful?'*

These questions only work when they are asked normally. If you are anxious, hide it. You are not saying *'I'm lost (or stuck), are you?'*, or *'Am I being in any way useful to you?'* So watch your tone and re-contract when the conversation is going well and not only when you have got stuck.

Stay in the present tense. When someone has just made a leap, *'Where are we now?'* enables you to catch up with where they are. As much as you might want them to describe *'What just happened?'*, you would be asking them to explain and inviting them to travel backwards to satisfy your curiosity. It might be useful to them, so ask: *'Is it useful to you to articulate what just happened?'*

Re-contracting questions keep the process on track and remind the thinker that this journey belongs to them and that you are not in charge of the direction. Checking in works well only as long as you are happy for them to say it is not useful! If this is all about them moving forward in their thinking, knowing whether they are moving forward makes the process more useful. Insight checking questions include:

- *'What have been your insights so far?'* and
- *'What do you know now that you didn't know when we started?'*

Watch your tone. You are not asking *'might I possibly have been of any use at all?'*

Timing is everything. The later in the conversation you wait to re-contract, the less likely you are to do it at all. This is because it turns from a question about the work to feel like a question about you: *'Was I any good today?'* Even the very best coaches have performance anxiety. But the work is not about you. It is about the process. Checking in is not about your performance. It is an opportunity to ensure that the exploring is serving the individual, their context and the contract that you co-created at the start of this conversation.

Re-contract or check in with as few words as possible. If you use too many words, you will stop the thinker thinking. If you check in lightly and need to change direction, you can work out how to do that together. As much as summarising is useful sometimes, getting the thinker to share their own insights about where they are now will be more useful than them hearing your insights about their insights – unless they have missed out something huge.

The contract is never the contract

Once you are in the middle of the coaching container, hold lightly the boundary of today's contract. Notice diversions and distractions. You won't know whether they are distractions or whether this tangent, or new thing, is a critical part of what needs to be explored. It is common for the rightsized agreement that you created at the beginning of today's conversation to begin to look like it is no longer the most important question for today. You will need to decide what to do together. Unless you co-create this, you are leading. This is their conversation. Ask them and if you agree this is new territory, then make a new contract, with a slightly reduced STOKeRS.

> Example: *'We seem to have started talking about your purpose at work and we began by talking about how you manage your time. What is our question now?'* (Subject)
> *'How will you know by the time we finish today that we have moved this forward?'* (Outcome)

You will need to decide whether a fuller re-contract, including K ('how will you know?') and a R ('how shall we do this?'), will give better focus to this re-contracting or whether they would be distracting. Just don't ask *'Where shall we start?'* this late in the conversation.

Rightsizing, or setting the contract for today, is like setting the ground rules. Sometimes you will need to renegotiate a brand new set for the next phase of your time together.

Not everything is useful

Etched in my mind is a career conversation. It was two hours long. We did a good clear contract at the outset, and the substantive part of the work we needed to do took time. We started at 12.00. It was 13.45 when I asked: *'Is this useful?'* The thinker answered: *'No!'* I can remember thinking that this might be the first occasion I would offer someone their money back. In case we could turn it round, I asked: *'What do we need to do in the fifteen minutes we have left so that it is useful?'* He told me. We did it. And at 14.00 I asked what insights he was taking away. *'This has been an amazing conversation'*, he said. *'So useful. Thank you'.* I hope that I managed to hide my surprise. This is another example of what happens when *'... the coach trusts the process more than they trust themselves'*.[5]

Models

Coaching tools and knowledge from books and courses might be valuable. And the tool with the greatest value in any conversation is the person you are with.

They will come up with the best questions. They will partner with you to have a great conversation that will serve their thinking. This only works when you are giving them all your attention and not searching around in your mind for the right question or technique. The first step towards more transformational conversations is to work less hard. Use your tools and models as your last resort not the first. Let the thinker lead. Starting with a model can mean you take the thinker to places that may not necessarily be valuable to them.

Tread lightly with tools. If you think a model or tool will be useful, ask the thinker and don't over-explain. It is for the tool to serve the thinker, not for the thinker to serve your tool. I see many coaches trying to fit thinkers into their models or tools rather than responding to them. This is not served by coaching courses which require written reflection asking coaches to include a certain number of tools in every session. Coach training is there to serve the people who will come to us to think.

There is an art to introducing things very normally and in a way that does not interrupt the flow of the conversation. Usually, it is in what the thinker is saying. Whilst observing some coaching, the thinker said: '*I just need to stand back*'. The coach had done some work around visual, auditory and kinaesthetic learning and asked, '*What will standing back look like?*' A stronger question might have been, '*Go on then – let's stand back*' and to have simply stood. Interestingly because they were already standing for the practice, the thinker listened to herself and not the coach and did take a step back. At that moment, those of us observing saw a significant change in her position and her face. She had had an insight.

I was benchmarking some coaches in an organisation, and the thinker was asking a question like do I stay or do I go? The coach was trained in neuro-linguistic programming (NLP)[6] and decided to use a timeline exercise. Ninety seconds into the exercise, I and the observers noticed the thinker had a huge insight. His face changed and his eyes lit up. The coach duly completed the exercise inviting the thinker to follow him for another thirteen minutes. By then, the thinker had lost the energy that the insight had generated.

Remembering techniques take up headspace and stop your full attention being on the thinker. What could have been done differently? First, watch the thinker all the time. Second, notice the insight, and ask about it, simply: '*And the insight?*' Third, it would have been useful to check whether that was enough – simply: '*Is that enough or is it useful to stand in other options?*' Finishing an exercise when it has done its work is serving the tool and not the person and their processing.

Be unconditionally positive about time

A plane flight can only end when the plane touches down. Extending the middle part of the flight may mean that you never land. The transformation that you seek in coaching might only come when you start to land the conversation.

When conversations get lost, it is likely to happen when you extend the middle. You don't seem to be getting anywhere, and you hope that giving a bit more time will bring some insight. You are thinking that you don't have time to do justice to the huge thing they have brought.

Rightsizing the question and using time as a partner in the process are two of the ways in which you can ensure that the conversation moves forward. And you need to sound like you believe it.

Given that we never have all the time in the world, time is a reality in every conversation. I observe an unwillingness in many cultures to talk about time at all. If you are going to use the time to bring a positive boundary to the coaching container, you need to know what time it is. Otherwise, you may well get lost in the thinker's stuff.

Smart phones and smart watches will not serve you well. You or the thinker may have a watch that you can see. There may be a clock in the room. Whatever you use, you need to be in control of the time and know how much time you have left. However big the thing they are talking about, stay positive and use the end time as your marker. In coach training courses, I notice how often the observer keeps the time even when I have given that role to the coach. Having a third party keeping time may get you to the tea break on time. The value to the conversation comes when you know the time, all the time.

| Example: | *'We have been talking for an hour'.* |
| Becomes: | *'We have an hour left – what do we need to do between now and then to get where we need to be?'* |

That is a process question. And half way through the conversation, we are beginning to land the plane.

Being stuck

The thinker might arrive at the conversation stuck. And one, or both, of you will probably get stuck at some point during the conversation. This is normal. Notice early. Getting stuck can feel like '*Oh dear*', '*Oh no*' or '*Oh help*'. It is easy to feel guilty and think that this is about you. It is not. If you were formed in any caring profession, you may be hard-wired to match body language and tone to create a good rapport with people. It's a core skill. When someone says something sad, you sit down, sit still, slow down and listen. Matching pace and tone like this are an excellent way to build trust and rapport. It also keeps people stuck. Using too many words can get them more stuck. Move!

Twenty years ago, I used to offer a half-day training about managing 'stuckness'. One day I was sitting in the noticing chair and observed that moving physically almost always moves the stuckness. If someone is going to move forward in their thinking and they are stuck, you will need to move. Match for rapport, mismatch for change is a principle widely taught in NLP. Sometimes you will mismatch intuitively. You need to mismatch pace or tone or position in order to move towards change and action. Try moving in your chair, leaning forward or slightly speeding up your words. And see what happens.

I was observing some coaches in order to give them feedback as they worked towards accreditation. One coach asked the thinker what they were bringing. '*I want to talk about how stuck I am*', they replied. The coach respectfully listened for some time, asking a Clean Language[7] question: '*Tell me about your stuckness*'. The longer the story went on, the more still they both became in their tone and position. Eventually, the coach turned to me and said, '*I don't know what to do, we're stuck*'. The stillness had facilitated trust. But it had not enabled the thinker to move forward. Physically moving can enable and allow someone to move forward in their thinking.

Move

It is deeply human and respectful to stay still when someone is being still. It is holy ground. And moving is useful to enable progress. You have at least three things that you can move and adjust: pace, tone and position. Adjusting one a little might be enough. And sometimes when someone is very stuck, it might be useful to adjust them all at the same time. Take your cue from the thinker and feel your way in.

Moving might look like anything from leaning forward in your seat and picking up a glass of water, to speeding up your voice, to becoming a little louder or quieter or even standing up and walking. Moving might be finding a different place to meet or to sit. We do what we normally do when we are where we normally are. If some of your conversations with a colleague are informing and others are facilitating their thinking, it may be useful to ensure that you have the different conversations in different places. When someone has brought something to coaching that they find difficult, after they have downloaded, I often invite them to move to another part of the room as we begin to explore how they can move this forward. In fact, I almost always coach standing up now (with the agreement of the thinker who also stands) because it makes movement a much more normal part of the conversation. For example, when they say '*I need to stand in a different place*', you can both move easily. Coaching standing is also useful because it is clearly different from other kinds of conversations. If you are going to do this, you need to find a normal way to begin that does not make the thinker assume this is strange.

Where the work happens

In *Challenging Coaching*,[8] Blakey and Day talk about coaching as a conversation that is high in support and challenge. This is where the work happens.

Blakey and Day state that people begin to change and grow in '*the loving boot*' Kim Scott[9] calls this '*radical candour*'. That is what coaching is all about.

When we are afraid of challenge, our conversations can be high support and low challenge. Blakey and Day call these encounters '*cosy*' because it is easy to get stuck there. *Radical Candor* offers a similar grid and Kim Scott calls this place '*ruinous empathy*'.

In the autumn of 2018, I did a straw poll of delegates on courses over a two-week period. There were 200 delegates, 196 of whom said that when they are the thinker, they like the conversation to be radically candid. The dilemma for moving to coaching is that about 150 of them preferred to facilitate conversations that Scott would call ruinous empathy. That is an interesting insight about the risk of conversations that are more led than they are partnership. If we lead people into a place that is high support and low challenge, we are demonstrating something about our belief in their ability to do the work.

Change the medium[10]

Einstein said that '*you can't solve a problem in the frame in which it was created*'.[11] Many problems have been created, to some extent or other, with words. People will come to conversations with us to think things through in a different way. The more we use words and talk together, the more the risk is that this looks like other conversations they might have had. Coaching is different. Doing things differently enables that to be clearer. Using fewer words will enable you to notice better.

A deeply simple way to explore complexity is to stop talking about the question and to actually look at it together from a distance. Standing back together engenders partnership. Both of you will notice things that are beyond the words you are using together.

Introduce a new medium normally and in plain language, noticing how it is received. Some people will begin to see things differently almost immediately, and others will hate it, and you need to move on. This is not about your personal preference. If you prefer words, someone who has come to think may find changing the medium useful. If you get excited as you read this, remember that not everyone you work with will share that zeal. Always ask first and always ask lightly: '*Is it OK if we try something?*' Never forget that your aim is to enable the thinker to keep thinking. The more words you use to introduce kit, the more you are interrupting the flow. Be brief.

If the conversation is going to move beyond transaction and get to transformation it is likely to happen here. When you move away from words, you are looking together at the question. The noticing is now doubled. And you won't be forming the next question.

Changing the medium from talking to each other with words to stepping back and looking at something together looks less like a counselling room or management meeting, and more like two people standing and looking together. It is a useful way to create new awareness.

SOGI

Visually mapping enables us to see a snapshot of the complexity and connections around the question that the thinker brings. Any encounter with airports and planes demonstrates a similar complexity with a system or constellation of all kinds of comings and goings to make a flight ready for the air. In coaching, we need to pay attention to what is going on in the wider eco-system because everyone lives and work in interconnected worlds of family, work, politics, race, gender, geography and more. These worlds are commonly called systems. Peter Senge and his colleagues describe this complexity by observing that 'everything is in connection'.[12]

Holding the systems in mind in the conversation is an important role for the coach. Without it, coaching at work can become more like Employee Assistance and may have less benefit for both the individual and the organisation.

A common acronym used to look at systems is SOGI.[13] It has been quoted in many academic theses, and I have not successfully found the original source. SOGI is a useful lens to have in mind in conversations to remind us that some of the connections around relate to:

- Society
- Organisation
- Group or Team
- Individual

Map it out

You will have your own ideas about changing the medium. Here are some that have worked well for others. All of these are a useful way of enabling the thinker to look at the past in the present. Make sure that the physical position you take to notice doesn't feel like they are showing their homework to the teacher!

A delegate on a recent course told us that her husband has a job that takes him all over the world. Every time he drives out of an airport in a hire car, he stops and looks back so that he will be able to know where he is when the airport becomes his destination later in the week. He wants a visual memory of where he will going.

As we navigate change and encounter new or similar situations, we look carefully, and we see what we see and think that's enough. Is it? Or do we focus too narrowly? When people are thinking about complex situations, they often miss the pattern or the connections. When they are able to see it from a distance and look round the corners, they can make sense of the vastness of their system quickly and generate a different point of view. Inviting them to map it out and look at it can change the conversation. They might want to depict the different systems they are in. Many people ask to take pictures of what they have done so they can continue thinking later. Professor Jose Luis Villegas Castellanos[14] noticed that drawing or making a pictorial representation relating to a problem in mathematics also contributes to its solution.

- Offer a pen and plain paper – '*Is it useful to draw as you speak?*'
- Use stuff – '*Do you want to map that out as you speak?*'

Use whatever is in the room. They could draw with pen and paper. I carry plain A3 pads and pens everywhere. Cutlery or items on the table in a café are great. I carry a pot of buttons with me because they are different shapes and sizes. So are coins. Whatever you use, the stuff begins to carry some of the information. Neither of you needs to hold it anymore.

Some guidelines:

- Ask permission before you start.
- This is about what you see and not about the story, so you don't need any detail at all – don't ask for an explanation.
- The thinker does the work, and you watch as they map their situation and challenge them to reflect on what they see. Ask them what they notice before you say anything about what you see. Notice dissonance more than detail. Say what you see without interrupting or diagnosing. Eighty percent of what you notice will not be useful, so be light in what you say. Twenty percent may be deeply insightful. They don't need to explain to you why it is insightful.
- Looking too closely at the picture is the same as getting too close to the story when you are talking. Learn to watch the eyes of the thinker as you offer an observation. This is where you will notice insights. Use very few words. This takes practice and may feel as unnatural as patting your head and rubbing your belly at the same time. You do not need to understand the situation. They need to see it differently.
- Don't touch their stuff – invite them to clear it up at the end.
- Introduce this during the exploring phase of the coaching container. Although they might say they would like to change the medium during the contracting, it is probably too early to offer it, especially if this is the first conversation you have had.
- Some people begin to use their arms as they speak – with them there's no need to ask permission – if you slide a pad of paper to them and hold a pack of pens they will just start using them!

Standing in a different place

Another way of exploring a complex situation is to invite the thinker to stand in different places. They could walk the situation out using paper to mark things on the floor. Sometimes simply asking them to move can be enough. Mats can be useful here because they provide a visual marker for different places or options. I use felt circles which I saw in some Coaching Constellations[15] training with John Whittington and Kirstie Papworth. When you are moving and the thinker is mapping their world on the floor, you hold the mats for them to place. You are not there to place them yourself. That would be leading. When they are following or watching you, you are leading. Check in with *'is this useful?'* If not, move on.

Standing in different places is great when the person has a number of different options. Standing on an option is an embodied movement that goes beyond thinking about it. This is a much-simplified version of the ancient tetralemma.[16] Offer a mat for each option and throw an extra one down for the thing they have not yet thought of. Notice together. Like the objects or drawing, you are noticing dissonance. For example, someone might stand on one mat and not on any of the others. Notice, don't diagnose – and say what you see. If this is useful, every thinker will use it differently. This is another example where you need to be brave and trust the process.

Mats are also useful to stand in someone else's shoes and look at a situation from a different place or time. A few times someone thinking about whether to stay in a job or to leave has taken a mat outside the nearest door and stood on it to see what it feels like.

Using kit does not work for everyone. You will notice that quickly and move on. And yet taking a different perspective can change the way in which the thinker begins to view a question, especially when this involves stakeholders and organisational culture and assumptions. It keeps you from getting stuck in the problem with them.

Use metaphor

If they are using words or metaphors to describe a situation, use them.

Example: They say: *'I'm all at sea'*. You might ask questions like *'What are you going to do with your ship?'*

Example: They use physical words: *'It's heavy'*. You might offer the nearest heavy thing to hold. Now they are experiencing in their body what they are thinking in their mind.

Use a metaphor if you sense one. And if you wait, they may well bring their own. Coach Claire Banham relates: *'The lady I was coaching yesterday decided that, as we were in the final ten mins of our session, she didn't "want to open the whole can of worms today". Then she paused and said, "so to finish I'd like a bite-sized worm please!" That picture was so useful, and helped her choose how we closed the session'.*[17]

Changing the medium enables people to perceive or to see things differently. Belgian playwright and poet Maurice Maeterlink said that '*it is far more important that one's life should be perceived than that it should be transformed; for no sooner has it been perceived, than it transforms itself of its own accord*'.[18] When someone sees something for themselves, in a new way, everything changes. They do not need you to make the meaning for them. When this happens, you will have no idea about what to do next. Ask them what they would like to do now. I offer that we could do something, or we could stop the conversation. Even if we are less than halfway through a conversation, if the perception is deep, we have done some great work together. Moving on to the next item on their list seems to be disrespecting the significance of the transformation – unless that is what they would like to do. Going and living with the insight might be the most useful thing for them to do.

Be normal!

Using kit works if it is not seen by the thinker as a weird technique. Introduce things simply. An internal coach in a large retail organisation said to me, '*I'm doing a lot of coaching at the moment with people who have worn out their words. Objects and other media are what they need to make new meaning*'.

Often using kit is more natural that you might expect. A manager on a one-day coach training said, '*This way of talking about things doesn't work for me. I need to chunk things*'. Looking around for anything normal and useful that I could find, I saw my purse. Grabbing a handful of coins, I said: '*Here you are, chunk them if that's useful?*' Immediately his face became less red, and he simply responded: '*That really would work for me*'.

The segue is simple and normal when you are responding to what you hear. A delegate in an Action Learning Set training folded his arms and said to the group: '*If only I could see it from a different place, I'd know what to do*'.

Two colleagues turned to one another: '*Didn't we learn a technique to do that on a course?*'

I intervened. '*What did he just tell you?*'

They looked at one another and then at me. '*Can't remember – but what on earth was that tool?*'

Pointing across the floor in the middle of the group, I repeated what the delegate had said: '*If only I could see it from a different place, I'd know what to do*'.

And he leaned back in his chair and began to look. And he saw. And he moved forward.

People talk about different media in the way they speak. The more you notice without forming questions, the more you will hear it and can invite them to do what they have just said. They tell you what you need to do together. This is another place to offer a '*Go on, then?*' question.

Changing the medium is a simple way of moving from just talking to looking at something together. This makes exploration more useful for the thinker and easier for you. It requires great noticing and few words, which enables the thinker to do more of their own processing. It is a great way to begin to be less reliant on notes.

Say what you see

Changing the medium moves you to looking at something together. The best insights for the thinker come when you say what you see. Describing what you see moves from observation to you affixing meaning.

Describing what you see:	*'So that's your team, and these big things are the senior managers'.*
Saying what you see:	*'Those seem close together, and colourful, and those three are very large'.*

Saying what you see is so simple that it is quite hard to do. Say it as a question. You might be wrong: *'That line has a gap?'*, *'That's solid?'*, *'That person has no mouth?'* The insight comes through the simplicity. British comedienne Joyce Grenfell[19] recorded a series of monologues based in a nursery school. In one, she is heard speaking to Caroline who has drawn a red picture. *'I wonder what it is?'* enquires the nursery teacher, *'Perhaps it's a lovely red sunset, is it? Or a big, red orange?'* From the tone of the monologue, you can hear the frustration of the imaginary child when someone gives meaning to her picture: *'It's a picture of Mummy! For a moment I thought it was a big, red orange, but now you tell me, I can see it is a picture of Mummy'.*

Let the thinker make their own meaning.

Working virtually

My coach training in the late 1990s was entirely on the phone. Virtual coaching has been a preference for some for their whole career – offering the opportunity to work from home. Covid-19 brought a change to working practice across the globe, moving everyone to working virtually for a while, and some for ever. As long as you are comfortable with it, the thinker is more likely to engage well. Don't apologise!

All the ways to change the medium described so far can be used when you are working on the telephone or via video link. The same rules apply. You need to be normal about it and to drop it if it's not bringing any new insight.

Moving is easier on the telephone than on video or face to face. A recent diary mishap meant that I had a coaching call when I was in London. We spent the hour on the phone as I walked along the quiet of Regent's Canal. It was interesting to notice how much my moving freed up the thinker's exploring.

Changing the medium works when you cannot see what the thinker is looking at. However, you need to believe that it will work for it to have any chance of being useful. This is an example of trusting the process more than you trust yourself. If you are unconvinced, try it out with a colleague first. As soon as there is complexity in what a thinker brings, I lightly ask if they have any stuff around in case it will be useful to look from a different place later in the conversation. While they are looking at their picture, I will map what I am hearing on my desk. Saying what I see might also bring new insights, if that is useful to them.

Putting in

There are disagreements between coach practitioners and professional bodies as to whether input is ever acceptable or not. I will not explore here the different views or what they are called. The powerfulness of a conversation comes, not from what you call it, but whether you have both agreed what you are doing and whether you have stuck to that agreement and negotiated together a slightly different way of working if that is useful.

If you are a line manager, mentor or supervisor, there may be an expectation that you offer ideas and input of your own sometimes. Some people may come to the conversation hoping that you will do that. For twenty years, my company 3D Coaching has been teaching people in organisations to use a coaching style. When we invite problem-solvers not to give advice, they almost always offer more. If you are a fixer or helper, putting in is normal behaviour for you. A couple of years ago, when training people to use a coaching style at work, we stopped asking people not to put in and started talking about when you put in and how much you say. This is all about timing and volume and is covered in mentoring in Chapter 8. Since we began to share this, people are putting in less, and facilitating their colleague's thinking more.

Moving to action

Sometimes actions or next steps emerge during the middle, exploring, part of the conversation. Equally, they might only become clear after you have begun the ending (Fig. 13). When actions emerge early, I ask people if it is useful to write them down. It might not be, and we do not want them to lose their insights on the way.

A colleague went on a management development programme where the facilitator drew a tombstone on the flip chart with the words: *'Knew it but didn't do*

Figure 13 Moving to action

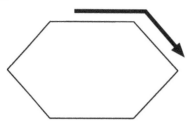

it'. The message was clear. Go out and put what you are learning into practice. Moving from exploration to action is an important part of the coaching process.

The optimistic and future-focused mindset with which we began the conversation assumes that alternative ways forward exist. Given that coaching does not have to be about solving a problem, the action from a conversation about complexity does not need to be a solution. Not everyone needs something else to do. Indeed, an action may be to do less. It might simply be enough to have a next step or a more refined question. Our role is just to work with the thinker to move forwards. Even one step is progress.

In *Experiential Learning,*[20] Kolb introduced his Learning Cycle and talked about how adults learn as they move between action, reflection, learning and trying things out. The next step from a conversation may fall into any of these or be an iterative movement from one to the next. In service of the thinker's development, we may need to challenge them to take a next step that is outside their comfort zone. For example, I might encourage someone whose preference is learning and reading to do something with what they already know rather than read another book.

Not everyone needs to plan their actions with you in the conversation. If the thinker has made a transformational shift as they have explored today, getting specific about action may not be necessary. As much as the professional coaching bodies advocate open questions, closed questions work better as the conversation nears its end. If the purpose of this phase of the conversation is to close the container, or land the plane, open questions risk taking off into a new conversation. Closed questions demonstrate that you are not inviting the thinker to report to you everything they will do, unless it is useful to them to say it out loud. The tone of the response will give you both useful information.

Questions like *'Do you know what you are going to do?'*, *'Is it useful for you to tell me?'* and *'Do you have the resources you need to do it?'* elicit one of three responses. A resounding 'yes' means that you can avoid using up their time reporting back to you. It is evidence that they have moved ahead of you, and may not feel a need to share that. This only needs a deeper exploration if you get a 'no', or more commonly a half-hearted sounding 'yeeees?' This is another example where the quality of coaching is indicated by what happens after the conversation and not by adhering to a script. Your ending will contain gaps and leaps and grammatical inconsistencies.

Real play

A transactional action evokes little energy – for example, it might be a list to take away. Transformational actions come from understanding something at a deeper level that will evoke a change in behaviour.

Many coaching conversations involve talking about conversations that need to be had. The output could be to list things to remember in the meeting. Inviting the thinker to try out the conversation with you can be more useful. This is more than having a few bullet points on a page. The words we think we need to say sound different when we say them out loud. In life, we only get one chance at a conversation. If it misses the mark, we spend many days, months or years dealing with the consequences. In *Thanks for the Feedback*,[21] Stone and Heen notice that although we judge ourselves on the intention behind what we say, others judge us on the impact with which it lands. Once the thinker has left the room, and gone to begin the conversation in real-time, they only get one chance to have it. The thinker will live with the positive or negative fallout from that for hours or even months.

Instead of talking about talking to someone, real play moves the thinker to a place where they hear themselves speak and notice the impact of their words and tone. It is safe to get words wrong because the thinker can have another go until the sense feels right. '*Tens of thousands of medical errors*', say the authors of *Influencer*,[22] '*continue to happen because individuals who may have practised drawing blood or moving a patient or reading a gauge dozens of times haven't studied and practised how to confront a colleague – or even more frightening – a physician* [or manager or bishop or ...]'.

Real play is a chance for the thinker to try out what they might say in a safe place – at different levels of intensity. Get them to do it now in the room or on the call. This conversation is not rehearsal, learning a script or role-play. In the spirit of Annotation 2 of the Spiritual Exercises of Ignatius of Loyola,[23] what you are doing could be described as bearing witness. Real play is like using the empty chair technique in Gestalt therapy,[24] where you introduce a third chair into the conversation. In Gestalt, the thinker imagines the person they need to talk to is in the empty chair and tries out the conversation. Like any strategy where you change the medium, this works for some people and not for others. When it is useful, the chair remains in the room until the end of the conversation. This keeps the imaginary person present. What is described here builds on learning through Peter Hawkins and John Whittington, and then many hours of using what I am learning and seeing what works and what does not.

In systemic practice, John Whittington uses a cataleptic hand.[25] Catalepsy is a rigidity in the body, and the coach holds out a fixed hand to represent the person who the thinker would like to talk to (Fig. 14). Unlike the Gestalt chair, which remains in the room, John pops his hand up from the floor to represent someone and then lets it down when they are no longer needed in the conversation.

Real play works when it is clear to the thinker when they are talking to the imagined person and when they are talking to you. You are not acting the part

Figure 14 Bearing witness

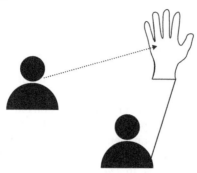

of the person they will be speaking to, and you do not respond. Standing at ninety degrees allows you to bear witness to the conversation as they try it out, without any confusion about who you are. You are clearly the coach. You will need to get beyond the 1990s slang phrase *'talk to the hand, because the face ain't listening'* because this can be useful to the thinker.

Moving into a different phase of the conversation like this needs to be safe for both of you. Stay clearly in the role of coach and keep out of fantasy. Ask permission in as few words as possible and be normal about it. You don't need to explain what you are going to do. That would interrupt their thinking. The cataleptic hand stops you absorbing emotion that does not belong to you.

> Example: *'Is it OK to try something different?'*
> *'Are you happy to stand?'*

Pop your hand up from the floor – stand between the thinker and with your hand at ninety degrees to them.

'Here is X' (point to your hand – they may need to start by talking to you, and then you move out of the way quickly)

'What do you really want to say to them?' (Nancy Kline says that *'thinking stops when we are upset. But if we express feelings just enough, thinking restarts'.*[26] This is decompression. Sometimes the thinker may need you to help them start off a sentence. This is raw emotion, not a script that they might really use.)

Check in: *'Any more?'*

Once they have decompressed, if that was useful, invite them to move to a new position and try it out again. We are not here to perfect a script. This is an opportunity to experience the impact of offering different levels of challenge and supportiveness.

Check in: *'How did that feel?'*

'Do you want to try another version – more challenging? Less challenging?'

Once we begin to move, I have a line in my head from least challenging to most challenging so that we can move up and down the spectrum if that is useful. Three tries is the most I have ever needed. Keep away from the extreme ends of the room. What they thought was a challenging attempt might need to be tried again with more challenge, and you will need enough space to move up or down the scale.

Real play offers an opportunity to try out Kim Scott's definition '*radical candour*', which means '*caring personally while challenging directly*'.[27] It can take a few attempts to get the balance right, which is why trying out the conversation live in the room with you makes sense. When real play is useful, you will probably see a visible shift in the thinker's body. If you are not sure, ask them: '*Is this useful?*' and find a way of moving on without apologising. Real play will not work if you are leading the thinker through an exercise which is not serving what they need in this conversation.

Move again

A common technique in NLP is to invite the thinker to imagine the future and think about the first step they took to get there. That requires a mind shift or imagination and words. A simpler version is to ask them if it is useful to stand up and move to a different place in the room where the future has happened and to physically look back. Given that the thinker is leading, you will be able to work out together what to do next in your conversation.

Inviting people to move enables them to try the action on for size. They can check out, with their body as well as their mind, whether the place they are aiming for feels right. The tetralemma in Chapter 5 is similar.

Binary options

It's common for people to get stuck in binary options. Either they can do this or that. This limits their way forward. Our role is to encourage the thinker to consider all kinds of '*what else?*' until no more emerge. When they come up with something and then dismiss it, challenge them: '*what would make that possible?*' Barry Johnson's Polarities[28] enable someone to see both perspectives at the same time. This can open up new possibilities, and is also useful when the thinker is stuck in right and wrong. Try exploring: '*So if you are both right, what now?*'

When they don't know what to do

The thinker may hope that you will tell them what to do. When I trained in coaching, people used to say, '*the client has the answer*'. Sometimes they don't. Perhaps a better saying would be that the answer is somewhere and I do not need to be the one who provides it. Sometimes the thinker does not know what to do and would like you to co-create ideas with them. When they have no idea, it is hard to come up with anything. Putting in the extremes can loosen their creativity:

> Example: *'You could do nothing? Or you could walk out today?* [or other extreme action given the topic] *What else could you do?'*

If you need to contribute a suggestion to encourage more thinking, be careful with your tone and volume of words. Ask permission: *'Shall we generate some options together?'*

Ensure equal participation, building on their ideas and don't sell your preferred option. As soon as there are enough ideas emerging, move from Senge's tell (Chapter 5) and ask them: *"Where are we now; what do we need to do next?"*

People bring things to think about when they are a bit stuck. Asking a question one degree of separation further away offers a new perspective and maintains optimism.

> Example: *'Is there anyone who can help you?'* [closed]
> Becomes: *'Who do you know who can help you?*, or even *'Who do you know who knows someone who can help you?'*

Asking the question from a different place enables them to access new information.

As you move to the end of the coaching container, changing the tone or the pace is a useful way to move to landing. There will be plenty of time left to do some more good work in the landing phase of the conversation.

Applying exploring at work

Moving is useful in meetings. Someone who had done our training shared that in a selection panel when the interviewers were unable to decide between the last two candidates, he invited them to stand and move to one end of the room if they observed that candidate A was a better fit and the other end for candidate B. If they were undecided he asked them to stand where they sensed they were. Everyone stood at one end. Their bodies were ahead of their minds.

Using drawing or objects can also be useful at work to communicate difficult messages to colleagues as you say what you see without judgement.

If you carry out review or appraisal conversations with others, getting them to use buttons to take an overview of their work can often help them to notice new and different things.

What will you do differently at work as a result of what you have read in this chapter?

Applying exploring for experienced coaches

If you are unsure about using any of these media, find another coach who is willing to try things out with you. Unless you trust the material, it is unlikely to work. All of this chapter is about you doing less and the thinker doing more.

When you listen to a recording, ask yourself: 'How much is the thinker thinking? And please don't use all of this chapter at the same time with the next person you coach!

What will you do differently in your coaching as a result of what you have read in this chapter?

Applying exploring for coaching supervisors

Using stuff is useful in coach supervision to enable coaches to see how their own personal process is showing up their relationships with those they coach. You can both look at what is going on from a different place.

What will you do differently in supervision as a result of what you have read in this chapter?

Notes

1 Association for Coaching (2012), *AC Coaching Competency Framework*, revised June 2012, available at: https://cdn.ymaws.com/www.associationforcoaching.com/resource/resmgr/accreditation/rclac/supporting_documenation/coaching_competency_framewor.pdf (accessed 27 March 2020).

2 European Mentoring and Coaching Council (EMCC) (2015), *EMCC Competence Framework V2*, September, available at: https://emccuk.org/Public/Professional_Development/Competence_Framework/Public/1Resources/Competence_Framework.aspx?hkey=ad98bd86-8bb8-4435-913d-5258f6774375 (accessed 19 March 2020).

3 International Coaching Federation (ICF) (2019), *Updated ICF Core Competency Model*, October, available at: https://coachfederation.org/app/uploads/2019/11/ICF CompetencyModel_Oct2019.pdf (accessed 18 March 2020).

4 Hawkins, P. and Smith, N. (2013), *Coaching, Mentoring and Organizational Consultancy: Supervision, Skills and Development*, 2nd edition, Maidenhead: Open University Press.

5 International Coaching Federation (ICF) (2020) *ICF Core Competencies Rating Levels*, available at: www.coachfederation.org/app/uploads/2017/12/ICFCompetenciesLevels Table.pdf (accessed 27 March 2020).

6 Knight, S. (2009), *NLP at Work: The Essence of Excellence*, 3rd edition, London: Nicholas Brealey.

7 Sullivan, W. and Rees, J. (2008), *Clean Language: Revealing Metaphors and Opening Minds*, Bancyfelin: Crown House Publishing.

8 Blakey, J. and Day, I. (2012), *Challenging Coaching: Going Beyond Traditional Coaching to Face the FACTS*, London: Nicholas Brealey.

9 Scott, K. (2017), *Radical Candor: How to Get What You Want by Saying What You Mean*, New York: St. Martin's Press.

10 Arden, P. (2003), *It's Not How Good You Are, It's How Good You Want To Be*, London: Phaidon Press.

11 Widely attributed to Einstein.

12 Senge, P. (2006), *The Fifth Discipline: The Art and Practice of the Learning Organization*, revised edition, London: Doubleday.

13 Source unclear but Christine Thornton refers to Society Organisation Team Individual, available from: https://www.thorntonconsulting.org/index.php?option=com_content &view=article&id=77&catid=2 (accessed 1 April 2020).

14 Ibid.

15 Whittington, J. (2012), *Systemic Coaching and Constellations: An Introduction to the Principles, Practices and Application*, London: Kogan Page.

16 Schoetz, A. (2017), *Tetralemma: A 3,000-year-old method for 21st century decisions*, available at: www.linkedin.com/pulse/tetralemma-3000-year-old-method-21st-century-andreas-schoetz/ (accessed 27 March 2020).

17 In conversation, with permission.

18 Boldt, L. (2000), *The Tao of Abundance: Eight Ancient Principles for Abundant Living*, London: Penguin.

19 Grenfell, J. (1978) *Nursery School Free Activity Period*, available at: www.monologues.co.uk/First_Ladies/Free_Activity_Period.htm (accessed 26 March 2020).

20 Kolb, D.A. (1984), *Experiential Learning: Experience as the Source of Learning and Development*, Englewood Cliffs, NJ: Prentice-Hall.

21 Stone, D. and Heen, S. (2014), *Thanks for the Feedback: The Science and Art of Receiving Feedback Well*, New York: Viking.

22 Grenny, J., Patterson, K., Maxfield, D., McMillan, R. and Switzler, A. (2013), *Influencer: The New Science of Leading Change*, 2nd edition, New York: McGraw-Hill.

23 Ivens, M., trans. (2004), *The Spiritual Exercises of Saint Ignatius of Loyola*, Leominster: Gracewing Publishing.

24 American Psychological Association (APA) (undated), 'Empty-chair technique', *APA Dictionary of Psychology*, available at: https://dictionary.apa.org/empty-chair-technique (accessed 1 April 2020).

25 Whittington, J. (2012), *Systemic Coaching and Constellations: An Introduction to the Principles, Practices and Application*, London: Kogan Page.

26 Kline, N. (1999), *Time to Think: Listening to Ignite the Human Mind*, London: Ward Locke.

27 Scott, K. (2017), *Radical Candor: How to Get What You Want by Saying What You Mean*, New York: St. Martin's Press.

28 Johnson, B. (2014), *Polarity Management: Identifying and Managing Unsolvable Problems*, 2nd edition, Amherst, MA: HRD Press.

6 | Simple endings

What the coaching bodies say

I began talking about actions in the chapter about middles. Actions and endings are explored together by the professional bodies. The Association for Coaching describes *'designing strategies and actions ... leav[ing] accountability with the client while following through on own actions and commitments ... maintaining forward momentum and evaluation'*.[1] The EMCC *'[a]ssists client to clarify and review their desired outcomes and to set appropriate goals'* before describing a lot of checking in, *'ensur[ing] congruence between ... goals and ... context'*.[2] And the ICF *'[p]artners with the client to transform learning and insight into action. Promotes client autonomy in the coaching process'*; *'partners with the client to summarize learning and insight within or between sessions'* and *'partners with the client to close the session'*.[3]

Ending the conversation in partnership is the only way to close the coaching container which we co-created when we began.

The end of our exploring

'We shall not cease from exploration', says T.S. Eliot in the poem 'Little Gidding',[4] *'and the end of all our exploring will be to arrive where we started and know the place for the first time.'* Every time you part, the thinker is in the same physical space in which they arrived. And yet when they have explored, had new insights, or even named out loud things they know that they have not before acknowledged, there is new knowledge and knowing.

You will have more confident endings to conversations when you have more clearly defined beginnings. If your subject for today was enormous with no boundaries, you might both have been wandering in the dark, and insights may not have been clear. When you contract well and have been clear what you were doing today, in this conversation, insights and movement are more likely to have happened.

To be fully in partnership, the end of every conversation needs to be co-created just as much as the beginning. When you lead on the ending of the conversation, it breaks the delicate dynamics of partnership, and it is likely that you have taken responsibility well before the end. Even when the work you have done is a renegotiated version of the one with which you began, like landing a plane, you need to land the conversation.

Landing the plane

Passengers on a plane know that they are coming into land because the pilot tells them up to thirty minutes before they arrive at the final destination. The crew start collecting rubbish, finishing their mid-flight tasks and making sure everything is in order so that they are all ready for touchdown. The fasten seat belts sign lights up, and the pilot announces: *'Crew prepare the cabin for landing'*. When the plane finally does touch down, it is not a surprise to anyone. No one is in the toilets or putting their bag in the overhead locker. They are fully aware of what is happening and preparing their minds for the next part of their journey.

On recent flights in and around New Zealand, one pilot invited the crew to prepare the cabin for landing while we were still over the sea. Another flew a small plane right through The Remarkable Mountains and into Queenstown. Both raised some anxiety, and we had to have confidence that they knew how to land the plane.

Landing a conversation means starting the end of the conversation before the thinker may have got new insights. Only as you come into land the conversation and co-create the ending, will more insights emerge. In the same way that the pilot, passengers and crew trust the plane as a container that will hold them, you and the thinker need to trust the coaching process. You need to be brave, hold your nerve and use time positively as a partner right to the end of the conversation. Transformation often happens in the last few minutes as you are touching down.

Ending in partnership

When people are new to this way of working, I observe a sense of relief from the coach that time is almost up. If we are going to end in partnership, the person with the perceived power needs to stop taking responsibility for the time. In coaching, that is you. Taking responsibility for the ending sounds like:

> Examples: *'Let's end there'.*
> *'We are coming to the end of our time'.*
> *'Let's pick that up next time we meet'.*
> *'That's too big for us to do it justice today. Why don't you bring it back next time?'*
> *'We only have five minutes. Let's leave that until next time?'*

Using the plane metaphor, these are emergency landings. You have stopped the conversation because you knew what the time was. They may not have been expecting it. When you take responsibility like this, the partnership that you worked so hard to co-create at the outset is gone. The responsibility and the power are now with you. More significantly, the person you are with is likely to do exactly what you have told them to do. They will stop thinking and come back to pick it up with you next time. To maintain a thinking space where transformation is possible, the end needs to be as much in partnership as the beginning. You co-created the space between you and have done the work together. Co-create the end.

This co-creation begins with rightsizing at the beginning of the conversation. Start counting down to the end from about halfway through in order to land well. This rightsizes in partnership what you still need to do together.

Examples: '*We have an hour left. Where are we now? What do we need to do in the next hour to get where you need to be?*'
'*We have five minutes left, what do we need to do to end well?*'

It is never too late for a new insight to emerge. Even when you feel that a conversation has been hard work, useful insights can happen right up to the last second and beyond. You will notice them when you are looking.

Closed questions enable you to land well. When you ask open questions towards the end, there is a risk of opening up a new subject without having closed the last one.

Anything else?

'*Is there anything else?*' is a question that is slipped in at the end of conversations in order to be supportive and ensure that you have done everything that you needed to do together. It sabotages the coaching container by moving to a new subject when you have not fully landed the last one. If transformation happens when a conversation is well contained, the container needs to be closed off. '*Anything else?*' risks opening up a new and potentially unbounded topic.

If it feels like you have finished and you still have ten minutes left, close off the first contract:

Example: Coach: '*Have we finished?*'
'*We have ten minutes left. Is there anything else which would be useful to think about?*'
Thinker: [They outline something else]
Coach: '*So what is our question for this ten minutes?*'
'*How will we know in ten minutes that we have moved this forward?*'

Hold your nerve

This conversation or relationship was not established to solve a problem. It was co-created to explore in a way that the thinker feels heard and gets new insights into themselves and their stuff that they did not have before. It is a fantasy to expect that any conversation will fully solve the problem. As much as our role is to enable the thinker to get new insights, more work will happen in the next few minutes, hours and days. As long as new insights are emerging, the thinker is on the way – moving from what they knew to a new place.

In *The Progress Principle*,[5] Teresa Amabile and Steven Kramer looked at the diaries of 238 employees across seven companies. They discovered that when people take small steps forward, it has a positive effect on their work performance. Any forward movement can create momentum. In conversations, people regularly talk about feeling stuck. Becoming unstuck does not mean finding a complete solution. It means moving from inertia or even feeling an energy in living with the inertia.

Whether you are confident that they are moving, or unsure, you need to hold your nerve right to the end. Transformation can happen up to the last second, and beyond. I observe many conversations ending with a version of: *'Have we done anything useful?'* The intention of that question is: *'Was I any good today?'* Great coaching is not about how good you were. It is about how well you co-created and then held the thinking space for your companion. Don't undermine the progress that has been made by asking questions that stem from your own performance anxiety.

A coach on a training course was beginning to trust the powerfulness of the thinking process and space she was co-creating with the thinker. She kept out of the way and was present enough for the thinker to have significant insights. She couldn't quite believe it was working, so her final question to the thinker was: *'Have we in any way solved your problem?'* Given that the conversation was about movement and not finding a fully formed solution, this is like asking a passenger on a plane *'Have we arrived at your final destination?'* when the intention of this leg of the journey from London to Australia was to get to Frankfurt.

The coach's panic reignited the overwhelm that the thinker had brought to their conversation – and left behind. The gift that we bring when we co-create the coaching container and hold our nerve through the conversation is to keep overwhelm out of the way for long enough for the thinker to get a different perspective.

Example:	*'Have we in any way solved your problem?'*
Becomes:	*'Have we moved your question forward?'* or *'Have we done enough work for today?'*

The best learning happens after the conversation is over

When a plane lands well, and passengers disembark the aircraft, they keep travelling. On landing, the pilot says: *'We hope you have enjoyed your flight and wish you well on your onward journey'*. There is no expectation that we will travel together for another flight, although we might. In the same way, the next part of the journey – and often the best insights – happen after the conversation is over, even when transformation has happened.

When we demonstrate coaching, we invite the thinker to sit out after the coaching while the group debrief what they are learning. In the five to ten minutes they are left alone, they always go quiet, or look away, or grab a pen and start to write. Returning to debrief together, they always say that they have had new insights since the coaching ended.

Coaching offers people a productive thinking space. Given that more work will happen in the minutes and hours after it is over, it is useful to negotiate together the best time in the day for them to meet so that they can keep processing. I have been working with a man for more than twenty years. We meet for an hour four times a year. The coaching begins when he gets on the train and starts to reflect. It continues while he goes for a cup of tea, then we meet for an hour. He takes more time to reflect and then travels home. He likes to travel to meet me because that is part of the space we create together. He does about seven hours' work each time we meet. I am there for one of those hours.

Think about where can you meet so that the thinker can stay and reflect when the conversation is over rather than go straight into another meeting. Talk about how long the conversation needs to be, and what will they go onto next. I prefer people to have less time with me and then have time alone to continue to process new insights rather than leave our conversation to head straight to another meeting. Without enough space, a significant amount of their insights that emerge from this co-created process will be lost.

CALF

What does landing the conversation look like? Like much of what is shared here, I am always learning from those I teach. A group in Leicester started thinking about what we need to do to close the container, and end well. They suggested CALF as an acronym. This can be a great end to any conversation, not only coaching.

C – Contract: '*Have we done what we set out to do (or the new thing that we agreed on mid-conversation?)*'
A – Accountability: '*Where do you need to be accountable?*'

This is different from suggesting that the thinker be accountable to you. With this question, they can choose to be accountable to you, and they may have a more useful place to go.

L – Learning: '*What are you learning?*'

If the first time you ask this is as the conversation ends, this question might feel to you, and to them, like '*Was I any good today?*' I often hear it asked in the negative: '*Did you learn anything?*' Notice the positive intention in the words. The end of the conversation is even more effective when you have begun capturing the learning together much earlier on. This emerges when it will, as well as through regular re-contracting (Chapter 4). Assume learning is happening and check in early. If the thinker isn't getting any new learning, you can agree on a different way of working together to get to new insights – when you have plenty of time left.

You will already have questions you use to land people's learning. These might include:

> *'What do you know now that you didn't know before we started?'*
> *'And the insights?'*

When you summarise at the end, you are taking the lead. You will summarise what you consider to be important. Let them lead, and you can add in anything you notice that they have missed out if that is useful. Clutterbuck and Megginson's[6] Four I's are a useful and different way to capture the learning:

> *'What are the **issues** we have talked about?'*
> *'What have been your **insights**?'*
> *'What are the **ideas** we have generated?'*
> *'What are your **intentions**?'*

Distinguishing between ideas and intentions is a useful way to articulate the distinction between what's been surfaced and what they will actually take forward. It nails actions softly. When you are working with someone who is a creative thinker, these two questions positively reduce 101 ideas to something realistic. When they dislike smart goals or objectives, these words are received more positively.

F – Finished?: *'Have we finished?'* or *'Is that enough for today?'*

Working in partnership includes everything right up to the last question. I always ask *'Have we finished?'* a couple of minutes before our time is up. Or when it is clear that we have completed the work we needed to do today – even when we have plenty of time left. When the conversation is over, it is over.

At least half the time the answer is *'Ye-e-e-e-s'*. My response is *'No? We have a couple of minutes left – what do we need to do to get to yes?'* There is time to do what is needed and next time the answer to *'Have we finished?'* is *'YES'*. This is another example of when the positive pressure of time increases the potential for transformation. Your job is to be brave, hold your nerve and not make this about your performance – or lack of it. Planes sometimes need to come into land more than once.

And the rest?

However well you have navigated this conversation together, it is a fantasy that you will have explored or dealt with everything. Your role was not to fully solve their problem. The thinker leaves, we hope, having felt heard and with new insights about themselves and their stuff. We have spoken and wondered and moved together. It is for them to apply their learning and complete the next part of their journey. You are their coach, manager, mentor or companion. They are well able to manage their own stuff. When they are not able to do that, we can coach it out – using a coaching style to enable them to work out where to take it.

Stay confident and believe that you are working with a resourceful human being.

Examples: *'And the rest? Do you know where will you continue to think about that?'*
'And the rest? Do you have somewhere safe to take this?'

There is no judgement about the volume or importance of what is left unresolved. This question does not tie them to bringing anything back to you. It leaves them the opportunity to take the rest anywhere – including to you, if that is useful to them.

Doctors and church ministers regularly report that the big thing emerges at the end – and that people will not tell you the real reason for coming for a conversation until they leave the room. A minister with over thirty years' experience said, '*I was taught that people only tell you what they really want to talk to you about when they are leaving. I believed that. And it became true because I never asked them how they wanted to use the time we had*'. Even when you ask at the beginning, some people will say what is really on their mind as they leave.

I see huge things coming up at the end of conversations every day. Our role is to treat it as being something normal and not to maximise it. We have a duty of care to ensure they are safe. That does not mean that we necessarily have to manage it with them.

Example: *'That's huge. Let's leave that and talk about it in our next conversation'.*
Becomes: *'Do you have somewhere safe you can continue to think about that?'*

Landing a conversation well is an art. Trust the process right up to the end. Even conversations that may feel to you that they have gone badly may, in fact, have been useful. Remember the career coaching conversation in Chapter 5?

Transformational change

When there has been a significant transformation, you might land the conversation, and the thinker won't have any idea where they are going next. We still need to end in partnership and close the container. You will only know how to do this when you ask them and work it out together: *'What do you know now that you didn't know before – and what will you do with that?'*

A man drove for two hours to meet me for some transition coaching. Twenty minutes into the conversation, something happened, and I saw that things had visibly changed. I asked him: *'What do we need to do now?'* I remember him stumbling incoherently, trying to make sense of his new insights. In our agreement at the beginning of the work together, he had talked about a number of areas he wanted to explore. Now we were in a totally different place. So I said what I observed: *'It seems like everything has suddenly changed, and you may need some processing time. We could work out what we need to do together here, or we could stop, if that's more useful?'* We stopped, and he went to a coffee shop with a packet of pens and a large blank pad of paper delighted that it was acceptable for him to do what was useful to him.

The twenty-minute man is an example of the process being as, or even more, useful than the presence of the coach. He needed to settle his new insights. Processing his thoughts without slowing them down by talking to me was, in that instance, the most useful thing we could do.

All the ending questions you may have learned about support and obstacles might be useful in some conversations but when deep change has happened the thinker may need to simply sit with their new knowing. In this situation a transactional question about actions would have sabotaged our conversation. Given that we are not mind readers, we always need to ask what we need to do now. When a significant change has happened like this, and you have seen or heard or sensed a light bulb – or in this case a Damascene flash, they might be ready to stop.

The thinker's sense of relief at understanding something in a new way may suggest that they know exactly what they now need to do. They might. Don't assume anything. Ask them because there are times when the transition from understanding what they need to do into knowing how to do it needs some support. Closed questions can be effective here: *'Do you know what you are going to do with that?'* may well produce a compelling 'yes'. If it does not, then you can move to pinning things down with a more conventional ending.

Examples: *'What are you going to do?'*
            'How are you going to do it?'
            'What do you need to say to who, and when?'

Don't pick up where you left off!

When the work we are doing together is in partnership, we are a travelling companion on a small part of the journey. If you landed the conversation well last time, you won't pick up where you left off. The thinker will have moved forward. So we need to manage the tension between starting from where they are now and reporting back. As much as we would like to know what has happened in the in-between time, some of that is purely curiosity. Ask them: *'Is it useful to catch up with what you did after last time?'* If it is, time-bound a pre-conversation or you will easily slip to storytelling.

Applying great endings at work

CALF and the Four I's can be useful to end all kinds of work conversations. Try using the Four I's to generate together any written output needed from meetings.

What will you do differently at work as a result of what you have read in this chapter?

Applying great endings for experienced coaches

What needs to happen for you to end in partnership? What do you need to put down? What do you need to pick up?

What will you do differently at work as a result of what you have read in this chapter?

Applying great endings for coaching supervisors

If the value of coaching is in what happens after the session is over, what does that mean for your supervision?

What will you do differently at work as a result of what you have read in this chapter?

Notes

1   Association for Coaching (2012), *AC Coaching Competency Framework*, revised June 2012, available at: https://cdn.ymaws.com/www.associationforcoaching.com/resource/resmgr/accreditation/rclac/supporting_documenation/coaching_competency_framewor.pdf (accessed 27 March 2020).
2   European Mentoring and Coaching Council (EMCC) (2015), *EMCC Competence Framework V2*, September, available at: https://emccuk.org/Public/Professional_Development/Competence_Framework/Public/1Resources/Competence_Framework.aspx?hkey=ad98bd86-8bb8-4435-913d-5258f6774375 (accessed 19 March 2020).
3   International Coaching Federation (ICF) (2019), *Updated ICF Core Competency Model*, October, available at: https://coachfederation.org/app/uploads/2019/11/ICF-CompetencyModel_Oct2019.pdf (accessed 18 March 2020).

4   Eliot, T.S. (1943), *Four Quartets*, New York: Harcourt, Brace.
5   Amabile, T. and Kramer, S. (2011) *The Progress Principle: Using Small Wins to Ignite Joy, Engagement, and Creativity at Work*, Cambridge, MA: Harvard Business Review Press.
6   Clutterbuck, D. and Megginson, D. (2016), *Techniques for Coaching and Mentoring*, 2nd Edition, London: Routledge.

7 Presence, partnership and power

What the coaching bodies say

In talking about the logistics and boundaries of the coaching relationship, the Association for Coaching looks at trust, respect and belief *'in the client's potential and capability'*. *'Managing self and maintaining coaching presence'* alludes to the delicate dance between two people which *'[d]iscourages dependency on the coach and develops the client's ability to self-coach'*.[1] When partnership is directly mentioned by the Association, it is in relation to the organisation, the individual and the coach, not specifically to every conversation.

The EMCC *'ensure non-dependence'* and demonstrate a *'belief that others learn best for themselves'*. They do not specifically refer to power apart from a reference to being clear *'so that client is empowered to make an informed decision to go ahead with mentoring/coaching'*.[2] Their reference to co-creation is about the relationship: where *'Coach and Mentor and client work together in a partnering relationship on strictly confidential terms. In this relationship, clients are experts on the content & decision-making level; the coach & mentor is an expert in professionally guiding the process'*.[3]

The ICF talks about partnership fourteen times in a four-page document which begins with *'the criticality of partnership between coach and client'*.[4] They specifically refer to partnership with the client at the beginning, the middle and the end of the relationship and the importance of partnership with other stakeholders. So far, the ICF is the only professional body to specifically refer to co-creating the beginning, middle and end of every conversation.

Partnership

In the last five years, my learning journey has moved from stance and presence to exploring more deeply what partnership means, what it looks like, and how it can enable more effective conversations. As a coaching supervisor, I have always reflected with coaches on what they observe and experience in their work, using self-reported data. Now I invite them to bring a recording with them once a year so that we can occasionally work with real, observable data. This enables us not only to reflect but also to look and listen together at how presence, partnership and power show up.

If you want to improve the quality of your conversations straightaway, record some conversations (with permission) and listen back through the lens of the dance of partnership. Listen to the thinker, not to yourself. They come first. After all, it is their coaching space that we have the privilege of observing together. Listen to what they say or don't say. Notice when they are still thinking. Listen to the dance for when the tempo changes and when you move in too quickly. Who is doing the work? Are you in pace with the thinker? Are you leading them? Have they leapt ahead of you? Are you working in partnership?

As much as reflective learning is useful, it is this real data that enables us to simplify, learn to pace well and work on our timing.

If coaching is to facilitate someone else's thinking (and not to solve their problem) in service of the question they bring, we have to work in partnership. When we lead, we are making ourselves the expert. Any implication of *'I'll tell you'* or even *'I'll lead'* implies *'I know better'* and that is taking power in a conversation. Partnership in coaching, I think, is about bringing ourselves to the room and doing enough and not too much. Co-creation means starting every conversation by rightsizing what we are doing today. When we start every conversation in partnership, we get to the heart of the matter sooner.

Travelling companions

The Oxford English Dictionary defines partnership[5] as *'association or participation; companionship'*. However different people are in personality, culture, biography or status, there is equality in a partnership. We work together in service of something else. If the differential in power is too great between us in the room, it can get in the way. This power is not about status. It is about whether we are partners and companions with them on their journey, and whether the thinker is willing to do the work.

When I was sixteen, I travelled to visit my brother in Germany with my cousin Andrew. He is older than me, and was in charge. He had never flown before. I had flown once. Andrew gripped the armrests as the plane took off, and I tried not to be affected by his anxiety, quickly realising that I was a more confident traveller than him. Good travelling companions, or partners, need to listen, to be brave and hold their nerve. Neither of us had been to Bremen before, or experienced a 1970s Northern European winter. We were going into the unknown together.

Even if Andrew had been an expert in aeroplane design, I would not have been reassured. He did not need to have a detailed knowledge of Germany or to have read a guidebook to Bremen, although some of that might have been useful from time to time. What I needed in my companion was someone who believed that we could work out what to do together. The environment was challenging. The city was an ice rink with few planes arriving or leaving. It was touch and go whether our plane would even land. On that holiday, I did not need the boys to tell me how they thought I should navigate the icy, snow-covered streets in my new cowboy boots with shiny soles. I needed them to travel patiently with me as I learned to slip-slide for myself.

Being a useful companion in conversations requires us to be present, work together in partnership, and share the power together from start to finish. The thinker has commissioned us to be a companion on their journey – they are not paying to come on our journey. Our hope or intention is that at the end of each leg of the journey they are in a new place. This means that we need to trust both our companion and the coaching process, and then to do as little as we need to do in order for transformation to happen. A confident and humble presence is useful. And if we are going to talk about presence, we also need to talk about power.

It's a dance

Coaching is a dance. If you try to do dancing to someone else, it is a mess. You will fall over each other. Trust will break down between you. And if they can follow you at all, they will simply have danced your dance. Equally, you might follow their dance. That is not partnership either. Partnership is co-created as each conversation emerges. It depends on us having enough respect between us for us to let them do their work. When you dance, you are in touch with your surroundings, body and mind. You gain muscle memory. The more you simplify your coaching, the greater your level of ease.

Coaching is not magic nor a panacea. Nancy Kline describes it as a thinking partnership.[6] We need to tread lightly like a dancer. When the coach works too hard, it doesn't work or, in the words of Ella Fitzgerald: '*You can try hard, don't mean a thing. Take it easy and then your jive will swing*'.[7]

The way the dance of the conversation shifts and changes, develops and emerges is an art. Have confidence and belief in emergent thinking. You need to sit comfortably with the unknown and travel with the thinker to make it known to them. Sometimes you will get it right, sometimes you won't. It's hard to learn dancing from a book. Partnership is learned in the coaching room. I teach partnership and presence with an improv teacher. In improv, or improvisational theatre, most of what happens is spontaneous and co-created by the performers. It is a great way for coaches to learn how not to have a fully formed plan, not to be in control, and to learn to navigate more by wisdom and instinct than by knowledge. This is a place to learn how to hold our fear and navigate our need for control, and the times we freeze inside because we don't know what to do next.

Dancing is about movement: moving and changing tone, pace and position is all part of the dance. The gift that we bring to coaching is the quality of the conversation, as we dance together. Throughout the conversation, we need to check in regularly that what we are doing is useful and that this is still the dance that is the most useful to dance. Even non-directive coaching like Time to Think[8] or Clean Language[9] is directive if we use it right through a conversation without checking in. The coach is taking responsibility for deciding to continue without asking. We don't have to finish the tango if we decide together that it is more useful to segue into freestyle.

In dancing, the partnership between the dancers gets the momentum going. The movement generated enables the dance as well as the skill of the dancers. Let the coaching process give its own momentum as you co-create the coaching container. Every time you don't know what to do, ask – non-verbally or verbally. The thinker is the primary source of inspiration in the dance. Asking them what you need to do doesn't mean you don't know how to do this. We only need to do enough for them to do what they need – the rest is theirs.

It's not a date

In contrast to a dance which looks full of movement and flow, coaching can look static. In fact, from a distance, coaching can look more like a date. If your first question is a version of *'Tell me about yourself?'*, they will do exactly that. That is not doing work together. It is getting to know each other. If this takes the whole of the first conversation, your companion will be learning, that is what coaching is. Coaching is not about getting to know someone, although we do get to know them. Coaching is about engaging together for the thinker to do some real and useful future-focused work. If learning about them and their context is important to the thinker, time-bound it as a pre-conversation.

Example: *'Tell me about yourself?'*
Becomes: *'Why don't you take ten (or whatever is useful) minutes to tell me about you and then we will work out what we need to do together'.*

Keep the responsibility in the middle

Partnership only works when the thinker takes responsibility for what they are learning and what they will do. We are the facilitator and provocateur. We need to hold the process, and not do too much, add too much or say too much. This needs us to keep the responsibility for doing the work firmly between us. Think of responsibility as a giant exercise ball. If you leave the responsibility with the thinker, they will be holding the ball and may feel overwhelmed, unable to see around or over it. If you take the ball, it will be difficult to pay attention to the thinker. Co-creating the conversation requires both of us to keep this metaphorical ball of responsibility in the middle (Fig. 15) – between the two of us.

Unless we check in regularly, it is a long way from the start to the end of the conversation for us to be taking responsibility for whether it is working or not. We are not mind readers, so we will need to ask the thinker how we are getting on.

Figure 15 The ball of responsibility

If it is your habit to pick up the responsibility that does not rightly belong to you, you'll find that at the end of a day of coaching conversations, you are carrying a heavy weight. In the *One Minute Manager Meets the Monkey*,[10] Ken Blanchard describes this as taking other people's monkeys home. A coaching style can be useful for managers and leaders who pick up the ball of responsibility too quickly. This is more effective for you, your colleague and the organisation, and stops you waking up in the night with colleagues in your mind and therefore in your bed. An NHS manager on a coaching course recognised that she always asked her colleagues a version of the question, '*What problem would you like me to solve today?*' She changed her language.

Example: '*What can I do for you today?*'
Becomes: '*What do we need to do in this conversation for you to feel able to move that forward?*'

All sorts of things can destabilise this delicate balance of who is taking responsibility:

- you working too hard
- the thinker not wanting to do any work
- doing your favourite technique
- offering suggestions and solutions without permission
- changing hats without asking
- controlling the agenda
- wanting to be helpful

Starts with them

For coaching to be effective, we need to be able to work in partnership and believe that the person here with us is able to do the work they need to do in order to move forward. To be their coach, we need to trust them and trust the container we have co-created. If we don't believe they can move forward, they need to look for a different coach. This belief needs extra attention when the thinker is being referred by a third party, and the story we have been told is that they are not able to change, or indeed if the story they are telling themselves is that someone else in the organisation does not trust them. Once you have started the work, and the external voices are quieter, this trust becomes simpler.

Full partnership in the conversation requires the belief on our part that the person we are with is robust enough to deal with their own stuff unless it turns out they are not. If that happens, we need to have a different kind of conversation about what other intervention might be more useful than coaching. Let's call this Thinker Power. In mental health, hope and agency are the words used to describe this. Hope and agency are about optimism; they have a future focus and recognise the importance of people accessing their personal power. Acharya and Agius describe '*the central tenet in recovery [as being] hope – it is the catalyst for change, and the enabler of the other factors involved in recovery to take charge ... Ultimately, hope is just as important in recovery from mental illness as in physical illness because hope matters in any situation*'.[11] When we demonstrate that we think someone needs help, we are inadvertently taking power over them. This reduces their personal thinker power. In his work on Transactional Analysis, Karpman[12] describes this as taking the role of rescuer. To demonstrate that we believe someone has agency and is robust enough requires less pity and more respect. '*Giving up wanting to help or rescue people is essential if you sincerely respect them*', wrote psychotherapist Bert Hellinger.[13] Thinkers, like coaches, are a bit broken. They also have robustness.

Call the Midwife[14] is a BBC drama about a group of midwives in London in the 1960s. In one episode the midwives are training young medical doctors to deliver a baby. The midwives always work in partnership, engaging with the mothers-to-be and calling them by name. The doctors are reminded to look at them and to treat each mother as an individual. Several times the doctors want to intervene and rescue while the midwives encourage them to keep calm and navigate some complex deliveries. The midwives trust the mothers-to-be, and the process of birth. They are companions who demonstrate the courage that enables the mothers to trust the process. In one scene, the midwife laid out all her tools and had a contingency ambulance in place. They did not need to use any of them. The mother managed to use her own resources as they delivered the baby together.

In conversations, it's easy to turn to tools and techniques, when the person we are with has all the resources they need. They need companionship while they access them. That only works when we can be brave, trust the process and manage our internal desire to help.

That episode of *Call the Midwife* reminds me of a comment made by Brené Brown on Twitter: '*I hoped faith would be an epidural for pain. Turns out to be a midwife who says "Push. I'm here. Sometimes it hurts"*'.[15] Perhaps another description of a coach is a midwife. We can't solve the other's problem. Our role is to stand with them with courage and challenge.

Ends with them

All the coaching bodies talk about ending conversations in relation to actions. So far, only the ICF talk about partnership at the end of every conversation.

Unless we work in partnership until the conversation is over, we have taken the ball of responsibility somewhere along the way. There are some ideas about what this looks like in Chapter 6.

Power tools

As much as studying coaching, learning models and having some great questions and tools in your kit can be useful, in the end, you are only a catalyst. Your role is to be a travelling companion who will bring challenge, support and companionship to the journey. You bring skills, your experience and your presence to a conversation with someone else who is far more experienced in their life and work than you are, even if they are not yet noticing it. Their expertise will always take priority over yours as you journey together. It is the co-created work you do together that adds value.

For my fortieth birthday, I did a charity trek across the Sinai Desert. They told us to travel light. We needed good boots, sun protection and plenty of water. One of the trekkers brought lots of luggage. It added no value and held others back. When you're not carrying your tools or trying to remember the guidebook, you will be more effective. It saddens me to notice the level of anxiety I see every day in coaches who have picked up along the way an assumption that they need to have learned the guidebook and be carrying a backpack of power tools.

Set questions and tools have a place. Like the midwife and the mother, their value comes after you have agreed what you're doing today, and only after you begin by using the thinker as the first resource. Timing is everything.

There are many one-to-one interventions where the expectation is that the practitioner has subject expertise. This gives them – or might look like they have – some knowledge and power. In sports coaching (which looks more like mentoring because the coach is probably a subject expert), the coach bases their feedback on what they know about sport (expertise) and what they see (real, observable data). The change and transformation in performance comes from the sportsperson choosing to apply what they are learning. Coaching is different. Even when you start the work together with some external data through psychometric testing or 360-degree feedback, the work you do uses more self-reported data and less real data than sports coaching.

An over-reliance on tools and techniques gives power to the coach. It might be useful to have some tools and techniques available but don't go looking for the right one because then you're not listening. If they could be useful, trust that they will present themselves later. We need to share the power, speak simply and avoid jargon. Fancy language might mean we are putting on clothes that do not belong to us. If we want to speak human to human, and maintain connection, both of us need to shed a bit of power. Make coaching your own and don't sound patronising!

It's not about you

The person you are talking to is probably having conversations with others and, we hope, doing some thinking themselves. Coaching is not about you. It is about the partnership you co-create while in conversation. This is their life and work. They will always know more about that than you do. Their stuff is not your responsibility. Your conversations with them are part of something bigger. If they are not engaging with others, that may be something useful to explore together.

I was coaching on a residential week in the Yorkshire Dales where people mid-career were reflecting on where they were, and how and what might be different in the next phase of their work. In the same way that the best of coaching happens in the spaces between conversations, most of the insights and transformation came as they walked, talked to each other or stared at the horizon.

Several times, I was asked how I decompress after having more than fourteen one-to-one conversations in forty-eight hours. The coach's role is to facilitate someone else's thinking, wondering and meaning-making. That doesn't need us to think, solve or make meaning for someone. We need to work out what we are doing in this conversation, notice well, say what we see and give the other our full attention while we are together. Much of what was said that week, I had forgotten by bedtime. It was not mine to remember, so I didn't take it in! In constellations work,[16] this is commonly described as 'facilitator's amnesia' where the work seems to reside somewhere other than in our normal memory. It is useful. In roles where we have responsibility for the stuff that is spoken about, we must take more in. But when the co-created conversation is all about someone else, they need our attention and presence more than our memory. That's why I don't take notes. This stance is another way to describe coaching presence. And when you don't take things in, you won't take them home either. They were never yours to take.

You may know a lot about coaching. That does not mean that you need to do more. You may know a lot about jobs like theirs. The usefulness of your conversation is not about that. A coaching conversation is useful when the thinker feels heard and has new insights into their own situation. We cannot give those insights to someone else. The most we can do is co-create an environment in which insights are more likely to happen. This will be useful sometimes and at other times it will not. We will never know if the work we are doing is useful unless we ask the thinker.

Coaches are human beings. We all remember having conversations that weren't going well, and all we wanted is for them to be over. Performance anxiety happens as much in coaching as any other kind of conversation. The further we get into a conversation, a question like '*Is this useful?*' begins to feel like '*Am I any good?*' So we don't ask it.

If coaching is about moving forward, '*Is this useful?*' is a necessary question throughout every conversation to ensure that we are doing what we need to do and to change direction if we are not. It is not about you. It is about whether the conversation is useful.

Underprepare

As much as you need to be prepared for every conversation, don't get too attached to what you pack for today's journey. The most significant tools are the two of you. Both of you bring useful luggage and some baggage. As much as it might be reassuring to you to be well prepared, having the tools in your hand may be overwhelming to the thinker. Expect the unexpected. The midwives laid out their tools with little intention of using any unless it was necessary. You need to be prepared, and you won't know what you need to do today until you ask the thinker because you are the material and need to model vulnerability, bravery and not being the expert in their stuff. Your role is to facilitate the process. This is what the professional bodies mean by '*using self as an instrument*'.

The preparation began when you learned to have conversations. Great coaching comes from formation – how you are shaped – as much as from information – what you know about our craft. We can have all the knowledge in the world, and we don't need to bring it in. Our preparation can be to reconnect with our inner knowing that this process works. And then to trust in our capability to listen deeply, work with what comes and choose together how to dance in service of what the thinker wants out of today – not what we may or may not think they need to work on.

Stance

Stance is about how we are inside and out. It is common to see thinkers trying to turn a coach into their manager, sitting face-to-face, hoping that someone else will fix their problem. Last time that happened, it was visible across the room. I invited them both to stand and continue the conversation whilst looking out of the window together. Moving to a 'being with' position from a 'talking to' place shifted the conversation and the thinker rediscovered her personal power and found a way forward.

One of the most significant pieces of feedback that I have received as a coach and a trainer of coaches was how the quality of my training improved when I admitted to a group that I am learning all the time. What I know about the art of conversation this week will have been tweaked next week by something that's been noticed that will reduce the work I do, simplify the process and make it more effective for my conversation partner. I recently spoke about the importance of partnership at a coaching conference. I think that I learned as much as the delegates!

The live coaching demo was done standing up. I always do that because everyone in the room can see, and also we know that people think faster when standing. The nature of the stage meant that we were standing at ninety degrees to each other (think two adjacent sides of a square). As she was talking and thinking, she was facing forward. I stood next to her watching her create some great ideas. And I only spoke when she turned to look at me. That clear invitation to me as the facilitator of her thinking to only speak when she invited me in by looking at me meant that it was easy to wait and not interrupt her thinking.

It worked on Tuesday, so we shared it in some training on Wednesday! It was so effective that Alex and I watched as someone accompanied a thinker. The coach's face suggested full attention and no question-forming. He was simply noticing and bearing witness. And then the thinker pointed to the floor as they moved to a new and useful insight. The coach turned and started to look at the same place on the floor. Now there were 100 degrees between them and they were looking in the same direction. The coach scratched his chin, and we watched as he got sucked into the stuff. The edginess was gone! I walked up behind him and silently tapped his arm to encourage him to move back to a side-on position. He stopped scratching his chin, and the edginess was back! Time and again over forty-eight hours we saw the value of that ninety-degree position which allows us to *be with* someone and shifts from the kind of position where we are *talking to* someone, and end up being seduced by the story. This is probably easier when we are standing up than sitting down.

Being with is a useful inner stance for coaches so that we can look, listen and notice together. Sarah Brisbane, a coach at Royal Papworth Hospital, says that this makes a coaching stance more like golf and less like tennis.

Be attentively not bothered

Coaching presence, according to the ICF and Association for Coaching, is a core competency of coaching. But what exactly is it? Two priests can lead church services using the same words. With one, you feel safe, and you can relax into the mystery of the moment. With the other, you are on tenterhooks. Something is missing. It is a presence. We cannot see presence. And we know when it is absent. In the poem 'Burnt Norton', T.S. Eliot puts words to what it is not, as he connects presence with a dance: '*At the still point of the turning world. Neither flesh nor fleshless; Neither from nor towards; at the still point, there the dance is*'.[17] Being fully present, at this still point in time in this conversation, means being neither too distant nor too close, neither too much nor too little, neither too bothered nor too disinterested. And yet our full attention – body, mind and spirit is with our companion. It is from this place of presence that we can co-create our working partnership.

When you think about times you have felt you had someone else's full attention, some of your experiences will be positive. You will also have memories of people whose attention was too present and too close. At those times, you may feel that you have neither space to breathe nor to process. How we are in the conversation is one of the deepest parts of coaching, and it takes time to inhabit this different way of being. In *Ash Wednesday* Eliot says: '*Teach us to care and not to care. Teach us to sit still*'.[18] This is the stance of neither from nor towards, of being fully present. It requires us to be fully attentive in the conversation, not to be in control or take onto ourselves what rightly belongs to the thinker. I call it being attentively not bothered. This is about courage and vulnerability. Sarah Broscombe, a coach and spiritual director, says that coaches need to *'get out of the way. Clear the space first and then step back in when they need you'*.[19]

Over-presence, instead of a co-creating partnership, can feel claustrophobic. It comes when we have a belief that the person with us needs help. Outside, it looks like leaning in and over-empathising or fixing and problem-solving. Inside it feels like *'Oh no'*, *'Oh dear'* or *'Great – here's a problem to solve'*. Inhabiting a space that is *'neither from nor toward'* requires us neither to drag our companion where we want to go, nor to lag behind when they have had leaps of insight. If you are a problem-solver and want to run the race with them, this can be experienced as leading. It is not your race to run. If you find yourself too close to the action in the conversation, it might be useful to move. Some of us can move an imbalanced power dynamic like this to partnership using words. Physically moving can be easier. You cannot be this present for too long at one time. It is exhausting. That is why it is unwise for full-time coaches to coach full-time.

Marianne Woerkom interviewed managers who were coaches in the same organisation. The thinkers *'attributed the effectiveness of their coaching to a large part to the relationship they had with their coach. Receiving unconditional acceptance and respect from the coach was not only a facilitative condition, but also directly responsible for change'*.[20] This is about trust and presence. It is interesting that Marianne's research recognised the need for a relationship that is neither from nor towards because, *'although there should be a certain distance between the coach and the coachee, a purely formal unilateral helping relationship is less effective than a mutual relationship in which a deeper personal connection exists between the coach and the coachee'*.

Helping

It is presence that has the power to unleash the thinking ability of someone else, whilst a desire to help or fix impacts both partnership and presence. Hospice doctor Rachel Remen observes that *'fundamentally, helping, fixing and serving are ways of seeing life. When you help, you see life as weak; when you fix, you see life as broken; and when you serve, you see life as whole'*.[21]

To talk about fixing and helping, we need to talk about power. Coaching is not about helping people. John Whittington talks about the importance of being *'useful, not helpful'*.[22] Coaching is about knowing how to hold the space in a way that enables someone else to think. In the same way that the aeroplane does much of the work in a journey, the coaching container (see Fig. 11) does much of the work in the conversation.

Mads Morgan, a coach with the Church of England, used to say that there is only a certain amount of power in a conversation. The law of conservation of energy in physics '*states that energy cannot be created or destroyed, but only changed from one form into another or transferred from one object to another*'.[23] If the coach takes the power, it must have come from the thinker.

Like any industry, the coaching profession has tribes – academics, practitioners, training providers, people who revere knowledge, people who revere practice, managers who coach, coaches who are trained or untrained, those who believe in qualifications, or accreditation, and who call themselves every kind of coach under the sun. Different tribes have different views about how much work the coach does and how much power they use in coaching.

Some tribes are perceived, or perceive themselves, to have more or less power than other tribes. This appears to contribute to the anxiety prevalent in the coaching profession that says: '*Am I any good?*' or '*Which tribe do I need to belong to that will make other people think I am any good?*' When you start coaching, you belong to a tribe. As soon as you discover that there are other ways of working, you will have guilt as you venture out. Maya Angelou, in a 1973 interview with Bill Moyers, said: '*you only are free when you realize you belong no place — you belong every place — no place at all. The price is high. The reward is great*'.[24] As you grow into yourself and find your own way, you will belong everywhere – and nowhere. This is not about being right or wrong. It is that we are all different.

The critical question is not about which tribe is right, but how do we best serve the thinker as they process?

Somebodies and nobodies

Robert Fuller describes this power play in *Somebodies and Nobodies*.[25] He calls it rankism – where we give people power – or indeed take it away from them. Fuller suggests that making ourselves somebody, will nobody others, and that somebodying others can nobody us. We learned some of this in the playground, so there is some unlearning to do here. This is a great example of power play, not power sharing. Describing this '*somebody mystique*', he says that once we have experienced excellence, '*something else happens, something mysterious. Our focus shifts from the accomplishment of the person, from the art to the artist, the dance to the dancer*'. This coaching thing subtly becomes about the coach who feels a strong pressure to perform, to be excellent, to add to the toolbox, to add value, and more. The ICF's observation that '*… the coach trusts the process more than they trust themselves*'[26] is an encouragement to focus on the space between us and not get caught up in our own performance. This takes presence – and practice. It's another example of the value of coaching supervision as a place to process and reflect.

While we think we add value by trying to add value, we won't add value – we will be taking more than our share of the process, or the space between. Music emerges in the space between the conductor, the orchestra and the audience. Transformation emerges in the space between the coach and the

Figure 16 Power sharing

thinker. Imagine what would happen to the music if the conductor did too much work?

Returning to planes, a successful flight is down to thousands of people. It's not just about the pilot. The whole process from ground staff and aircraft designers onwards is what makes travelling work. Coach Lesley Cave says that she is always '*fascinated at airports by the system or constellation of all the comings and goings to make that flight ready for the air. Coaches need to [trust and] pay attention to what is going on in the wider system*'.[27]

Great coaching is co-created in the space between the coach and the thinker. It is about the process in this time and in this place. It was never about you.

We can learn to not to somebody ourselves by not taking the power in the coaching relationship (Fig. 16), and to operate as much as we are able to with enough equality of power between us. However, if the thinker gives us the power, by nature of any reason – our biography, gender, academic training – they have somebodied us and nobodied themselves. Respect and power look different across culture and family hierarchies. There will be times when we have every intention of sharing the power and get somebodied. Naming that, by saying what we see, and asking what we need to do takes what is happening out of the shadows and into the space between us.

External power

In individual coaching, the thinker will contact the coach directly. As much as there are presence, power and partnership to be navigated here, the one-to-one conversation is fairly simple. The spider's web of presence, power and partnership is more complex as we engage with the wider system with all its stakeholders who wish to be part of the conversation.

Part of the complexity is addressed by good contracting for the relationship. This contracting is covered well in training courses. STOKeRS works well here – adapting the contracting questions for the long relationship rather than today. We need to acknowledge that money is power and will impact our presence if we need the work to pay the mortgage.

Power dates: The Chemistry Session

When coaching is commissioned by a third party in an organisation, it is common for the coach to be invited to have a Chemistry Session. This is an opportunity for the thinker to meet and choose between a handful of different coaches. It can feel like a beauty contest without any criteria for making a decision. If the thinker has had coaching before, they are more likely to go direct to someone who has been recommended, so most people who come to Chemistry Sessions are new to coaching, too.

Some coaches have the inner stance that we do what we do in the Chemistry Session and if that works, and the thinker decides to work with me, that's great. And if they choose another coach that's great too. This is a great demonstration of coming to a conversation from presence – or internal personal power. When we – or the coaching company – need the money, the date can become about outside power beginning with what is said, which is usually about your biography or authority, right down to power dressing. Too much power and the date falls over – too little, and we don't get beyond our first date.

We are human. There is a risk when we encounter high-status power that we match it because we think that is where our power comes from. The most significant thing you bring to coaching is your presence and how you do what you do. We need to match status a little but it's presence that does the work. Like the fable of the Emperor's New Clothes,[28] it's not the outside power that matters.

If the Chemistry Session is a power date, we need to recalibrate when we start the coaching. You will need to lessen your power so as to encourage the thinker to lessen theirs as they begin to display vulnerability and courage. This recalibration is a significant change of gear from your first meeting, and it can take a couple of sessions to get there. If outside power is important to the thinker, they may wonder what they have done. When you coach in contexts where this is true, you may notice the deepening balance of power across sessions as you move to a place where you can do deep work.

You will only know how and when to shift gear when you ask them. That will require a level of trust between you that comes from being neither a somebody nor a nobody. Coach Jenny Williams observes that many workplaces don't talk about trust even though a lack of trust may be causing the pain points.

You will both need to shed some power to be yourselves so that you can do some good work together. A changing gear question I heard in training was: *'I wonder if you're bringing some power to this conversation that belongs somewhere else?'* When we coach *somebodies*, their somebody is being nurtured by many *nobodies*. The coach's role is to match so that we can move in the coaching room to a way of being power equal enough. Here are some questions that may be useful to start:

Examples: '*What needs to happen for there to be enough trust for us to do good work?'*
                     '*What needs to happen for you to feel you can be honest?'*
                     '*Is there anything else that we need to talk about to be able to do the work?'*

Think about where you meet to disrupt the power dynamic. Do they come into your space? Do you go into theirs? Do you go for a walk? If the coaching is to be different from other conversations they have, you need to do something differently.

Remember that a Chemistry Session is two-way. Does the thinker want to do the work? Do you believe they can? Do you, or will you be able to, trust them? When I meet people to see whether they want to do some work, I do some coaching with them so that they can experience how I work. I call it triage, and charge for it.

Being empowering

When I ask people what they want to be different by the time we have learned about coaching, a desire to better empower others comes up every time. We accidentally disempower when we try and help, solve or fix, or do the work for them. I am a volunteer with the Motor Neurone Disease Association. MND (or ALS) is a disease that gradually causes weakness in the whole body. People lose their ability to move and speak, and it is nearly always fatal. My experience of being with friends with MND is that their personal power, or agency, can be the only thing they have left. Empowerment enables people to access their own power – however little they have.

Coaching gives people the means to take more control. Our role was never to solve their problem. Offering questions with your solution: *'Have you tried this?'* can add to their feeling of powerlessness. *'Would a few ideas be useful?'* keeps the choice with the thinker.

To dance well, we have to acknowledge the positive role that power plays as well as recognising the need to neutralise it. Coach Sarah Broscombe says that *'there is a wide recognition that powerlessness and disempowering is bad but a refusal to accept that the counterbalance must be true that powerfulness can be good. Empowering yourself is part of empowering other people'*.

As I write this chapter about power, I have been filled with a sense of not knowing enough about power. As much as I recognise that not knowing does not belong to me, and that it is a strong dynamic that I am picking up from the wider system, it is taking an enormous amount of effort and external support to hold my nerve. Power dynamics are everywhere. Coaching is simply two human beings talking together about one of us. It is not about someone who is more sorted out helping someone who is less sorted.

What we call the people we work with

Empowerment and respect start with what we call the people with whom we work. I am grateful to the man who articulated this to me at a public sector coaching conference. The organisers had asked me to do the closing keynote address and talk about the simplicity of coaching, weaving some of the learning from the day into what I said. This gave me the opportunity to listen in on other sessions through the eyes of the delegates. The opening session shared interesting research about coaching, supervision and mentoring. The talk and the slides spoke a lot about coaches and coachees, mentors and mentees, and supervisors and supervisees. We were asked to raise our hands at various times through the presentation to say which of these were names we owned. The man next to me sat still throughout. At the end, I asked him how he had found the session. He told me that he had a general interest in coaching and mentoring: '*I am not any of those things … and I am certainly not an "ee"*', he said.

There are hidden power dynamics in language. What we call the people we work with matters. We are simply people who have conversations with other people. The traditional client/coachee language of the coaching literature feels strange when you are using this approach with a colleague. I have seen a coaching style work between colleagues regardless of status as much as it works with people looking for external thinking support. This way of working changes lives and organisations. So what can we call the people we work with that demonstrates partnership and respect?

I acknowledge that in a book or a training context, we need to call the people we work with something, but what we call them impacts our inner stance. A client, according to the Oxford English Dictionary,[29] is '*a person under the patronage or protection of another… a person using the services of a professional person or organization; a customer of a person or organization offering services … a person receiving care or treatment from a counsellor or therapist*'. This does not feel like a definition of someone who is robust enough to engage in their own thinking process. Equally, the description coachee feels like a diminutive version of the coach. The robust human being with whom we are in dialogue does not belong to us. They are a resilient and resourceful human being, not '*my client*' or '*my coachee*', or '*my difficult coachee*'. It is not ideal, and I am still looking for a better word but for the time being, and for the purpose of this book, let's call them a thinker. I am interested that although thinker was introduced by Nancy Kline in the 1990s, it is not commonly used.

Power seats: How we sit

Coaching is different from other conversations. Everything we do needs to be different from the start, or both of us risk slipping into what we normally do – because people do what they normally do when they are where they normally are.

The position of the chairs in most coaching rooms can make it look like something else. The 120-degree angle you put between the chairs might make it feel less like an interview, but if the person who comes to see you has had therapy, and this feels like a therapy room, they may begin to treat you as their therapist. Similarly, it can feel like a GP surgery, a manager's meeting with a direct report – or even a date. This is a 'talking to' position. There are also associated levels of power in us that come with the different roles we play in our lives.

As much as we are here to talk and listen, we are also here to do some useful work together in service of their question. When the thinker talks to you, it's likely that a lot of stories will come out that may not give them any new insights. So where you meet matters. If you are going on-site to someone's office, try to use a room that they don't regularly use. If there is no choice, at least get them to sit in a different chair.

Example

Some hospital consultants had been trained to use a coaching style for peer support of more junior colleagues. The best place for them to meet was in their consulting room at the end of a clinic. It was a confidential, safe space. When their peers came, the conversations were not as effective as had been expected. All morning – and perhaps for many years – the consultants had sat in the chair of expertise. Their colleagues arrived and sat in the patient's chair. It didn't work because their colleagues felt like patients.

The energy required by the consultants to have a different kind of conversation whilst in the same chair lessened their capacity to be fully present. After we had talked about it, the consultants changed chairs before their peers arrived and were more able to coach and have a different kind of conversation when they sat in a different place. If you have a number of roles or wear a number of hats with a colleague, having different conversations in different places can make it much clearer what you are doing when.

Power sharing

When we are over-helping, trying to solve or analyse, the partnership between us is impacted. Dr Rachel Remen notes that *'helping is … not a relationship between equals. When you help, you use your own strength to help someone with less strength. It's a one up, one down relationship … When we help, we may inadvertently take away more than we give, diminishing the person's sense of self-worth and self-esteem'.*[30] Partnership needs enough equality. That is why it is so important to talk about power. It is everywhere in every conversation – who does the work? Who speaks first? What do we call each other? Who takes the notes?

There are power lines everywhere – gender, race, role, personal power, class, height, education, professional background, sexuality, accent, country of origin and more. The list is endless. I could introduce myself in many different ways: I am a human who facilitates other people's thinking; a business owner; a mother; a friend; a volunteer; a master coach with over 11,000 hours of coaching experience; an author; a former teacher and third sector worker. Every one of these is true. And with each one, you may assign power to me which I do not deserve, or indeed take it away because I have not said a whole list of other things which you perceive to be important. Hawkins and Smith[31] talk about authority, presence and impact. These are all received as power – or not. Authority is what we bring from our biography and experience; presence is how people experience us and impact is the combination of the two. When we get this balance right, we can establish trust.

My first manager had a wooden carving on his desk. It was a hand holding an egg. The carving represented a Ghanaian proverb: *Power is like an egg. If you hold it too tight, it will break. If your grip is too loose, it will fall.* Being aware of how our power comes across and using what we have wisely is an important part of establishing trust and partnership. This is another example of the value of supervision as a place to reflect on our presence and power. We may be aware of our inequalities, but how comfortable are coaches talking about our power and how aware are we of the privileged groups we are in?

'We tend to talk about race inequality as separate from inequality based on gender, class, sexuality or immigrant status. What's often missing is how some people are subject to all of these, and the experience is not just the sum of its parts', says Kimberlé Crenshaw,[32] professor of Law at Columbia and UCLA. This is called intersectionality, which is a lens for seeing how different inequalities interconnect.

Rachel Weiss is a coach. She is black and a woman. Some of the groups she belongs to are privileged. Some are not. Rachel says: 'I'd love all coaches to have done an exercise about which groups they belong to that are more privileged. And which groups do they belong to that are less privileged? If they have never talked about this before they'll freak out when people talk about race. Being in touch with situations where we are less privileged – will redress the power imbalance and help us to empathise with others'. We need to acknowledge white privilege and cultural differences.

Coaching works best when there is enough equality of power between the people who are talking to each other. There may be a differential in role, intersectional or personal power, but in the room, we need to find a way of being power equal enough in the conversation. That is about trust. When I feel that I am doing too much work, talking a lot, fixing, or taking power to please them, we are not power sharing.

Money is also power, and coaching is an industry. Continuing to work with someone brings repeat business. We need to be willing to let a thinker go when they can think without us.

Process power

Conversations are powerful when we have agreed together what we need to do in each and every conversation, when we are competent to do that and when we do what we have agreed to do, unless it is useful to do it differently, in which case we negotiate what that might be like. When I meet somebody who wants to do some work with me, I ask them what our conversations need to be like to be useful – without using any labels. The potential for misunderstanding is high if their definition of coaching is different from mine. It does not matter what you call it; coaching is simply a conversation where someone feels heard and gets new insights into their own stuff that will make a difference to how they think or feel.

While the obstacles may be in the power differences, effective power is in the process. Telephone coaching is useful because it removes some of the visual inequality between us. Either of us can choose whether to divulge race or sexuality. Some intersectional differences cannot be hidden.

Coaching is one way of having a conversation. There are many other ways. Tools and techniques offer status and confidence to the coach. But it is the work that happens in the space between that gets results – not what the coach does. I hear coaches talking about 'using self as instrument'. That is important and when taken too literally increases person power. When we trust the process, the space, the thinker, the process and the coach all need to be partners in the process. Perhaps using the space as instrument is something where we need to pay attention.

We are human beings. We know how to talk to people. It is how you do it that makes all the difference in coaching. When we give people space to think, they get new insights.

Building trust

All the professional coaching bodies talk about the importance of trust and respect. I notice how coaches take time and patience to build this up. That's useful. Except when the person you are working with has chosen to come for coaching, already trusts coaching and therefore trusts you.

When trust is already present, taking time to slowly build it up is your agenda and can train the thinker that the relationship is more about storytelling than doing the work. Kim Scott[33] describes conversations as being on continuums of caring personally and challenging directly. Staying in trust-building longer than is necessary for this partnership demonstrates more about high care '*ruinous empathy*' than getting on with the work, described as '*radical candour*'. You will not know if you need to take time to build trust unless you ask them.

Most coaches are observant enough to notice when trust is not there. Moving to an assumption that there is enough trust, and only taking time to build rapport if not, is useful because getting to new insights quickly enables the thinker to trust the process more. What will it be like when we see thinkers trust the process as much as they trust the coach?

Be clear. If getting to know the thinker is important, be clear with yourself and them that this is a pre-conversation and that you will start doing the work next time. When people come to coaching because they want to, I get straight on with the work having asked: '*Is there anything we need to talk about before we begin so that you trust me enough to do this work?'* The answer to that is almost always *'No – let's begin'*.

Trust, care and challenge raise questions of ethics if you are being paid to coach, and you have decided to take a long time to build trust without checking it is necessary. If you believe that no useful work will be done until session four, that is probably what will happen. What do you do if the thinker gets what they need in session one or two when the organisation expects to pay for six? When you trust the process and the thinker, you will discover that many people can get on with some useful work very quickly.

When it's not partnership

Some people who come to coaching arrive by choice. They know that this will be a useful piece of development for them. Others have been told, or recommended, to come on this journey by someone else. In order to move forward, they will need to do the work. The coach's role is to facilitate small pieces of that journey, to trust them to travel the path they discover, and to notice when they don't. They, and others, will measure success by where the journey leads not by what you do.

Coaching is about moving forward, although glancing back can be useful sometimes. If the conversation that is needed is to have a good look at the past, that will need a different conversation with a different kind of practitioner.

If someone does not want to do their own work, the best coaches in the world cannot make change happen. But dependency can be seductive, and there will be times when we will feel the pressure from the thinker for us to do more, know more or offer solutions. There is discomfort in discovery. And we are not working in partnership when we are doing all the work. The more work we do, the less they will do. Your conversation will only be transformational when you believe they can move forward. Not everyone who comes for coaching wants to be there. This can happen when coaching is commissioned in organisations. Some will have been sent or see it as a performance management tool.

If coaching is not useful to the thinker, or if they do not want to engage, talk about it:

Example:	[You work harder and harder in order to make this work]
Becomes:	*'Is this useful? What do we need to talk about before we can do some useful work together?'*
And in extremis:	*'You don't need to be here. We can stop the coaching if you would like to. We will need to decide what we are going to say to [the sponsor]'.*

We need to talk about this. Otherwise, we think we are doing a bad job. And while we are making it about us inside, they will make it about us, and it will become about us.

Coaching does not work when the coach works too hard. We have to be willing to name that and to lose the customer. This is also partnership. Them leaving is a choice. It is not your failure. And it is not your responsibility alone to communicate that *you didn't do a good job*. It is more likely that coaching wasn't the right intervention at this time. That's why the responsibility to communicate what's happened is shared. When coaches are working as associates, there are external power pressures that make us feel we need to make this work. When that is what we are experiencing, it makes partnership difficult to co-create. This is an ethical question. Do you continue to do the work come what may? And what is the impact on your confidence as a coach? The reputation of coaching as a process? Roger Steare's *Ethicability*[34] offers a useful filter to use when you are thinking through ethical questions like this.

I support coaches in an organisation to work more simply. In a survey of colleagues who had been theory trained and were not using coaching, they were asked what they would find useful development to build their confidence as coaches:

- How do I keep them engaged?
- How do I deal with their imposter syndrome?
- How do I build self-confidence in the coachee?

I think that these uncover an assumption that it is the coach's responsibility to make a change. You can't build confidence in people when they perceive that you have the power, or indeed when you think that you might have it yourself. That is not partnership. When we are working in partnership, the best way to manage these concerns and gaps is simply to ask the thinker. '*Coaching is not the golden capability it's made out to be*', says Hayley Gosling who managed the coaching programme in NHS East Midlands Leadership Academy.[35] The status of being a coach can bring some power that it does not deserve. It is simply a conversation. It is not for the coach to have all the answers. We facilitate the thinker doing the work.

A final note about partnership, presence and power

We need to trust the space we create together. We need to trust the process. We need to trust the person who has come to talk and believe that they are robust enough to deal with their own stuff. And we need to trust ourselves. Ultimately coaching is simply an extraordinary conversation where two people have a deep, human encounter to enable the thinking of one of us.

Applying partnership, presence and power at work

How do you need to be in conversations with colleagues to ensure that there is enough partnership between you to do your work? Where will it be useful to talk more explicitly about trust?

What will you do differently at work as a result of what you have read in this chapter?

Applying partnership, presence and power for experienced coaches

We don't know whether we are working in partnership unless we get external feedback or an honest self-reflection on observable data. Listen to a recording of your coaching – or indeed someone else's. This time listen for the dance. What's the rhythm? Who is leading? Where have you parted too much and where are you stepping on their toes? Notice where the thinker is tolerating you and where are you working in full partnership. What is the learning for you there?

What will you do differently in your coaching as a result of what you have read in this chapter?

Applying partnership, presence and power for supervisors

How are you already paying attention to partnership, presence and power in the supervision you offer? If it is not your practice to use real data with those you supervise, think about whether you might use recordings occasionally so that you explore partnership together by paying attention to where the power is in the conversation. With coaches in associate relationships, where do hidden loyalties – to the coaching company or the sponsor – impact the delicate balance of partnership, presence and power?

What will you do differently at work as a result of what you have read in this chapter?

Notes

1 Association for Coaching (2012), *AC Coaching Competency Framework*, revised June 2012, available at: https://cdn.ymaws.com/www.associationforcoaching.com/resource/resmgr/accreditation/rclac/supporting_documenation/coaching_competency_framewor.pdf (accessed 27 March 2020).
2 European Mentoring and Coaching Council (EMCC) (2015), *EMCC Competence Framework V2*, September, available at: https://emccuk.org/Public/Professional_Development/Competence_Framework/Public/1Resources/Competence_Framework.aspx?hkey=ad98bd86-8bb8-4435-913d-5258f6774375 (accessed 19 March 2020).
3 European Mentoring and Coaching Council (EMCC) (2018), *EMCC Competence Framework Glossary*, revised, available at https://emccuk.org/Public/Professional_Development/Competence_Framework/Public/1Resources/Competence_

Framework.aspx?hkey=ad98bd86-8bb8-4435-913d-5258f6774375 (accessed 19 March 2020).

4 International Coaching Federation (ICF) (2019), *Updated ICF Core Competency Model*, October, available at: https://coachfederation.org/app/uploads/2019/11/ICF-CompetencyModel_Oct2019.pdf (accessed 18 March 2020).

5 OED Online (March 2020), Oxford University Press, available at: https://www.oed.com/start?authRejection=true&url=%2Fview%2FEntry%2F34954%3Frskey%3D1cRCh8%26result%3D1%26isAdvanced%3Dfalse#eid (accessed 1 April 2020).

6 Kline, N. (1999), *Time to Think: Listening to Ignite the Human Mind*, London: Ward Locke.

7 Oliver, M. and Young, J., writers (1939) 'Tain't What You Do (It's the Way That You Do It)'. Song. First recorded by Jimmie Lunceford, Harry James and Ella Fitzgerald.

8 Kline, N. (1999), *Time to Think: Listening to Ignite the Human Mind*, London: Ward Locke.

9 Sullivan, W. and Rees, J. (2008), *Clean Language: Revealing Metaphors and Opening Minds*, Bancyfelin: Crown House Publishing.

10 Blanchard, K. (2000), *The One Minute Manager Meets the Monkey*, London: Harper-Collins.

11 Acharya, T. and Agius, M. (2017), 'The importance of hope against other factors in the recovery of mental illness', *Psychiatria Danubina*, 29 (suppl. 3): 619–622, available at: www.semanticscholar.org/paper/The-importance-of-hope-against-other-factors-in-the-Acharya-Agius/273258cf5aa86562875fcfd2c9492cde5ae9c1ad (accessed 27 March 2020).

12 Karpman, S. (1968), *Fairy tales and script drama analysis*, available at: www.karpmandramatriangle.com/pdf/DramaTriangle.pdf (accessed 27 March 2020).

13 Hellinger, B. (2016), *Love's hidden symmetry*, available at: www.familyconstellations-usa.com/wp-content/uploads/2016/01/Loves-Hidden-Symmetry.pdf (accessed 27 March 2020).

14 BBC (2019), *Call the Midwife*, Series 9, Episode 4, London: BBC, available at: https://www.bbc.co.uk/programmes/m000dv1m (accessed 1 April 2020).

15 Brown, B. (2017), *Twitter @BreneBrown*, 3 May (accessed 1 April 2020).

16 Heard through constellations teacher Lynn Stoney, with permission.

17 Eliot, T.S. (1943), *Four Quartets*, New York: Harcourt, Brace.

18 Eliot, T.S. (1930), *Ash Wednesday*, London: Faber & Faber.

19 In conversation, with permission.

20 Woerkom, M. (2010), 'The relationship between coach and coachee: A crucial factor for coaching effectiveness', in S. Billett (ed.) *Learning through Practice*, 256–267, Dordrecht: Springer, available at: https://www.researchgate.net/publication/226925328_The_Relationship_between_Coach_and_Coachee_A_Crucial_Factor_for_Coaching_Effectiveness (accessed 27 March 2020).

21 Remen, R. (undated), *Helping, fixing, serving*, available at: www.awakin.org/read/view.php?tid=127 (accessed 27 March 2020).

22 Whittington, J. (2012), *Systemic Coaching and Constellations: An Introduction to the Principles, Practices and Application*, London: Kogan Page.

23 Sarton, G., Mayer, J.R., Joule, J.P. and Carnot, S. (1929), 'The discovery of the Law of Conservation of Energy', *Isis*, 13 (1): 18–44, available at: www.jstor.org/stable/224595 (accessed 1 April 2020).

24 Angelou, M. (1973), 'A conversation with Maya Angelou', *Bill Moyers Journal*, 21 November, available at: https://billmoyers.com/content/conversation-maya-angelou/ (accessed 1 April 2020).

25 Fuller, R. (2004) *Somebodies and Nobodies: Overcoming the Abuse of Rank*, New York: New Society Publishers.

26 International Coaching Federation (ICF) (2020), *ICF Core Competencies Rating Levels*, available at: www.coachfederation.org/app/uploads/2017/12/ICFCompetenciesLevels Table.pdf (accessed 27 March 2020).

27 In conversation, with permission.

28 Andersen, H.C. (2019), *The Emperor's New Clothes*, Odense: H.C. Andersen Centret, Syddansk Universitet, available at: https://andersen.sdu.dk/vaerk/hersholt/The EmperorsNewClothes_e.html (accessed 27 March 2020).

29 OED Online (March 2020), Oxford University Press, available at: https://www.oed. com/view/Entry/34279?redirectedFrom=client#eid (accessed 1 April 2020).

30 Remen, R. (undated), *Helping, fixing, serving*, available at: www.awakin.org/read/ view.php?tid=127 (accessed 27 March 2020).

31 Hawkins, P. and Smith, N. (2013), *Coaching, Mentoring and Organizational Consultancy: Supervision, Skills and Development*, 2nd edition, Maidenhead: Open University Press.

32 Coleman, A. (2019), 'What's intersectionality? Let these scholars explain the theory and its history', *Time*, 28 March and updated 29 March, available at: www.time. com/5560575/intersectionality-theory/ (accessed 27 March 2020).

33 Scott, K. (2017), *Radical Candor: How to Get What You Want by Saying What You Mean*, New York: St. Martin's Press.

34 Steare, R. (2009), *Ethicability: How to Decide What's Right and Find the Courage to Do It*, London: Roger Steare Consulting.

35 In conversation, with permission.

8 Simple conversations in real life

'*You have to learn about coaching*', said the coaching sponsor to the senior leadership team, '*I know you're not going to be coaches, but this will impact every conversation you ever have again*'. The simplest principles of coaching can be applied across a series of conversations, and indeed in conversations that are not coaching. Co-creating can improve the quality of almost every conversation we have.

So far, the focus of this book has been on working simply and creating a container in a single conversation to establish the conditions for us to do some transformational work. Let's look at what the principles look like when they are applied in different contexts, from formal coaching to the doctor's surgery.

Coaching over time

Whether you will be meeting for two or twenty conversations, creating a container for the whole relationship is useful. This means that you will have a big container for the relationship as well as smaller ones that you co-create in each session.

When you meet to talk about the relationship, using your endpoint as six months after the coaching is over (Fig. 17), focus on the outcome – or sustainable impact – rather that what actually happens in the coaching. STOKeRS can be adapted like this:

Figure 17 Coaching over time

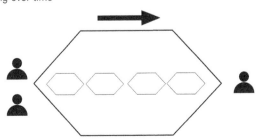

Example

S: What are the questions you are bringing to this process?
T: In the time we have, where do we need to focus?
O: What would you like to be different six months after we have completed our work?
K: How will you know six months after we have completed our work that this has been useful?
R: How shall we work this together?
S: Where shall we start?

The endpoint will vary from person to person. And in exactly the same way as a one-to-one, some people will not be able to answer the questions yet. It is still useful to begin to rightsize the work.

Partnership means that as much as you are holding lightly to the big contract for the relationship, you will need to co-create every conversation. Hold the big contract respectfully and lightly, asking them each time: '*where are you now?... [and] ... what do we need to do today?*' Coaching over time is more likely to be transformational when we are holding the list lightly and not ticking off an agenda.

People will bring things that are outside the contract. If you're unclear as you finish a session how it fits with the big contract, ask the thinker: '*How does what we are learning today fit with our long-term goal?*' Remember that the whole process is a dance. You'll pass the things that were in the contract at some point if they are still present when you get there. And you don't need to cover them in order – especially not *your* order. Sometimes you'll wonder whether someone is avoiding some of the deeper work. When that happens, ask them: '*Are we avoiding ...?*' This is an example of coaching being direct and not directive.

Coaching, like dancing, is about momentum. If there is little movement, and the thinker hasn't put into practice their actions from the last session, ask them: '*What did you do instead?*'

Notes have a place in coaching over a number of sessions. Ask yourself what they are for. This will be a good indication of what you need to keep and what you never need to write down. Data protection legislation is an encouragement to keep only what is necessary. Notes may keep you on track with the big contract. And coaching is about moving forward, so it is useful to remember that there is a risk when looking back on notes before a future session that you are doing exactly that: looking back when the next conversation is to look forwards.

Third and fourth party work

External coaches working for organisations are likely to be commissioned by a third, fourth or even fifth party. For example, the COO would like one of their direct reports to have coaching. They ask HR to commission an external coaching company to provide a coach to someone coming to think. The coaching company commissions a coach. That is five degrees of separation. The wider the distance between the original real data and the coaching conversation itself risks that the key players are passing to the coach responsibility that is rightly theirs. Contracting well is critical. And it will never be clear enough.

When the organisation is paying for the work, the organisation has both investment and responsibility in the process. They want outcomes that are useful for them. And they need to play their part in the development of their colleague. Three- or four-way contracting meetings are useful. In Chapter 5 we looked at SOGI as a simple way of naming just a few of the layers of the systems people work in. In multi-way contracting for organisational coaching that might mean considering Customer/Service User, Organisation, Group or Team, and Individual.

In a multi-way contracting meeting, the closer the participants are to working with the thinker, the better. They all have their part to play in the development of their colleague. It is not simply down to the coach and the thinker. Without multi-way engagement, there is a risk that the coach is being used by the organisation as a rescuer.[1] And our role as coaches is not to save the organisation from doing the work it needs to do.

I remember a phone call from the head of an organisation asking whether we would coach James. He gave me a list of about five things that needed to be tackled in coaching. '*Have you told James any of this?*' I asked. James had been told nothing, and distance made a multi-way contracting meeting impossible. I politely told the CEO that we would be unable to accept the commission unless he had spoken to James. The next day I was copied into an email to James that outlined what I had been told. It followed up their conversation and listed the bullet points that the CEO wanted James to work on. When I spoke to James, I asked him what he needed to know to trust me, and then we began to talk about the list. James said: '*It's none of those. They are symptoms. The thing I need to work on is this*'. The thing was deep, long-standing and might have been served by coaching or therapy. Given his self-awareness, we agreed to try coaching and see how it went.

Multi-way contracting meetings will almost always involve presenting the symptoms. The coach and the thinker need to pay attention to the things that have been part of the commissioning contract. And those things are rarely the actual thing that needs attention.

Example

What other interventions are happening with this individual and their team? Where does coaching fit into those?

S: What is the focus of the coaching?

T/O/K: Six months (or whatever is appropriate) after the coaching is over, how will you know that it has been useful to the individual, the team, the organisation and the customer?

R: What part do you need to play to support the individual in their development?

(S: Where to start is entirely between you and the thinker.)

Midway through coaching, or indeed even more regularly, you can re-contract with the system in mind:

'We have had half our coaching sessions. Where are we now?'
'What else do we need to do to make sure that this is useful for you, your team and the organisation?'

Manging confidentiality and who feeds back to whom – or not – is well covered in coach training courses. Supervision is important for all coaches and essential for coaches working in complex contracting situations. Self-supervision is useful too. Mapping out what you see by changing the medium with pen and paper or objects can enable you to begin to notice what needs attention before you start the contracting and then the work.

Triage

It is common for people to present needing, or asking for, a series of conversations, and for it to be unclear to them and their line manager/chaplain/HR adviser what the best form of external support might be. External support costs money and some interventions have waiting lists. When the person eventually gets into the room, it may emerge that they needed a different kind of support. Coaching as triage can be useful here.

Triage in a coaching style starts with the premise that everything someone might bring to the conversation is normal and that they are robust enough, or have the agency, to manage themselves. If it emerges during the conversation that they are not, that gives some useful information about what other intervention might be useful. Contract (using STOKeRS) at the start of a single-session, thirty-minute conversation. The purpose is that this person will be able to rightsize their question and work out what the best kind of support for them would look like. This leaves the responsibility and the control with them. You are not there to dig deep and do the work – simply to be a confidential space to facilitate their thinking about what the work needs to be. Listening without diving in is empowering to them, especially if the coach is someone outside of their system to whom they can be honest.

Your role is to hear them and to notice what they are saying. You might reflect the headlines and underbelly of what you are hearing. Name what is. Don't dig in. Notice with them their capacity to move forward. Help them scope

the options and work out how they can access that support, if that is useful to them. Options that come out of triage might include:

- saying it out loud in this conversation being enough
- journalling/thinking alone
- talking to a friend
- finding a coach
- finding a counsellor
- finding a therapist
- finding an adviser
- finding a mentor
- seeking medical help

Coaching may turn out to be the best next step. Whether it is, or not, this single session will have enabled them to begin to move forward. That is a gift.

In the car in Bolivia

The gift of a place to think in a coaching way can emerge in all kinds of places. As part of his day job, a coach went on an international trip to Bolivia. He was visiting marginalised ethnic communities with Cataquil, the inspiring and humble CEO of a partner organisation.

As Cataquil drove him through lush green countryside, the visitor asked him about his vision for change. This moved into an impromptu coaching session about his vision and the strengths he was bringing to his new role as CEO. Cataquil moved from feeling that he was not a man of vision to an 'aha' moment about life not being about material wellbeing. From there, he progressed towards a clear sense of his calling to help the youth of a marginalised group to escape from their vicious cycle of poverty. He said he went to bed that night still pondering this new conviction.

Cars are great places to coach because they naturally put us in a *'being with'* position. This is similar to the walking coaching described in Chapter 4.

Using coaching in other roles

Coaching is useful as a leadership style in all kinds of roles. The secret is to be normal and absolutely avoid any form of *'can I coach you?'* That sounds like you are doing something to someone. In many organisations, as soon as you use the word coaching, people go into the mindset that you are the expert. So segue into this different kind of conversation in plain language without using the word coaching. That might sound like *'would some thinking space be useful?'* When they have experienced it, colleagues who value a coaching style will begin to ask for it. There is no need to explain what you are about to do. Your colleague is not an unwilling participant in a magic show. You are simply going to talk in a slightly different – and yet totally normal – way.

Over the last year, I have been looking for volunteers through Twitter. I recruit people who don't know what coaching is who are willing to have a fifteen-minute conversation with me that will be recorded to be used in training. The purpose at the outset was to be able to demonstrate competencies to coaches in training by showing what conversations are really like – not what it looks like when a coach coaches a coach. What I am learning is that the right-sizing questions are so normal that you can just get on with the work without explaining anything at all. And they always say what a surprise it was that we went so far so fast.

When it is appropriate, a coaching style is a useful way of moving from a big chair/little chair conversation where power is given to, or taken by, the person in the metaphorical big chair. If the big chair is your natural style, or your colleague naturally takes the little chair, a coaching style is likely to raise suspicion. Ask them: *'Is there enough trust between us to be able to have a useful conversation in a different way?'*

Five minutes

You might be standing at the coffee machine or the water cooler when someone comes up to you and tells you that they are stuck, downloads onto you or asks you to fix something. This is a great opportunity to have a quick coaching-style conversation. You might have more conversations like this than formal coaching sessions sitting down with the door shut.

Here are some ways to segue into coaching by inviting them to think. Five-minute conversations will be started by your colleague, so that you will know the subject.

> Example: *'Would you like to think that through now?'*
> *'I have five minutes if that's useful?'* (Time)
> *'In five minutes' time, how will you know that we have moved this forward?'*(Outcome and Know)
> If the question is vague, asking *'How can I …?'* (i.e. how can they) will rightsize the question.
> *'Where shall we start?'*

Standing up will speed up the thinking. Five minutes only works if you are positive. *'I have five minutes'* feels very different from *'I only have five minutes'*. Unless you talk about time, they will not know that you are not about to walk off. Five minutes is a long time if you avoid inviting them to explain the problem. *'What's your question for this five minutes?'* is useful here as long as your tone is invitational! If you are in a public place and physically contain the space, for example, you both turn slightly towards a wall to keep others out, that will also contain the conversation.

Closing lightly with CALF might sound like:

C – *'So you wanted X, where are we with that now?'*
A – *'What will be your next step?'*
L – *'What are you learning?'*
F – *'Are we done?'*

Only if you need more time, will you need to look at diaries. The thinker may already have moved forward their question.

Mentoring

Although coaching and mentoring are quite different in purpose, the coaching container can be particularly useful in mentoring conversations. Mentoring is often a longer relationship, and the quality of the relationship is as important as the quality of individual conversations. When I am the mentor, I know something you don't know, and I'll tell you if it's useful to you. At one end of the coaching spectrum, no knowledge is put in. Mentoring is further across the spectrum because a mentor comes with a variety of wisdom, knowledge and networks that might be useful. The container can significantly improve the quality of mentoring conversations. The most effective mentors know when and how much to put in.

In mentoring, we both need to know what the question is before we offer any answers. Returning to Keith Webb's[2] definitions of coaching and mentoring, we

Figure 18 Putting in

need to *draw out* before we *put in*. Where input is useful, a drop or two of information is more effective than a tsunami. Rightsizing the question means that the input is the right size and shape (Fig. 18).

When we give input, ideas or advice too early, we unintentionally make ourselves the expert and are saying to our colleague that we think they don't know. Timing is everything. Let input be your last choice rather than your first choice. Englemann et al.[3] observed that the brain switches off while it is taking in advice. When this happens, the advice does not embed in the neocortex, which is good insight that even in mentoring the thinker should be doing most of the work!

On reading a blog post by David Clutterbuck about testing and exploring in mentoring, I recognised that the coaching container could be expanded for mentors. The first time I used this was with headteachers in a mentoring programme for aspiring heads. Knowing that the value of input is in the timing and the volume, it turned out that they did not need to offer any input at all. Combining Hawkins and Smith's[4] CLEAR, Clutterbuck's blog post and 3D's coaching container illustrates visually the steps that can make a mentoring conversation transformational. The output of this is CLE (TE) AR:

Contract:	Rightsize the question for today.
Listen:	Look, listen and notice.
Explore:	Dig deeper.
Drop in:	Now you are clearer on the question, input can be useful, with permission. Before I introduced the watering can a few months ago, this diagram had a syringe to indicate where in the conversation to offer small drops of input, with permission. In a learning day, my colleagues pointed out that if we talk the language of noticing and not diagnosing it was ironic that the diagram includes a device used to treat disease! Watering cans provide just enough water to enable growth and development.
Test:	Ask them: *'Now you know that, what do we need to do here?'*
Explore:	Explore again now they have some input to work with.
Action:	
Review:	

Watching people use this as they practise mentoring conversations, I observe that data is not always needed. Ask them: *'Would it be useful if I offered something here?'* Sometimes input will be essential: *'I'd like to offer something here'.* Unless there is only one way, this is an opportunity to scope out some ideas. Try not to sell your preferred option.

Example:	*'I think you should do this ...'*
Becomes:	*'Some people do this, some people do that, some people do something else. Now you know that, what do we need to explore together here?'* and you return to exploring. It is not unusual at this moment for the thinker to come up with their own, even better idea.

It is easy to slip into offering good ideas without asking whether that is useful. Artist Andy Leek leaves handwritten posters around London called *Notes to Strangers*.[5] One note reads: '*Think of the last bit of advice you gave and see if it's useful to you*'.

When it is asked for, and when it addresses the thinker's question, advice can be useful in mentoring. And sometimes what we offer to others is, in fact, what we need to be hearing ourselves. Offering to listen might be even more of a gift than offering solutions.

Changing hats with consent

At work, we wear many hats which have different names. Peter Senge, in *The Fifth Discipline*,[6] describes a continuum from telling to co-creating: *Tell – Sell – Test – Consult – Co-create*. This moves from '*I am telling you what to do*' to '*I might put something in if it's useful*' to '*we are doing this together*'. Other hats might include supporting, pastoral care, supervision, performance management and more.

What we call a conversation doesn't really matter. What matters is that we have a conversation that is useful to our colleague and that in it we do what we have agreed to do in service of them and their context. Whether you call that mentoring or coaching, or indeed something else, it is clarity about what we are doing that will enable the conversations to be most effective.

Telling conversations are instructive. There is a feeling that adding information and advice adds value. It demonstrates that you know something. Telling is also quick. Sometimes it is the right thing. I was doing some online development of coaches in Bangladesh after earthquakes in the region. We were using audio because the internet connection was poor. In response to the coach's question about what they wanted to do in the conversation, the thinker said: '*I want to think about how to manage in an earthquake*'. I interrupted and asked whether that was right now or ever? It was right now. This was a moment to tell, not to co-create. We stopped the call so that they could leave the building. If someone needs information, tell, unless coaching is useful first to clarify the question so that you can give the most useful answer.

Selling conversations influence and persuade. In coaching and mentoring, even if offering ideas has a place, including a sales pitch about why the ideas are good does not. All it does is to take the focus from the thinker and put it onto you and your story.

As you move along Senge's continuum from tell to co-create, conversations take longer and engagement increases. Test is offering a few ideas which you have thought about earlier in order to get a sense of which will be a good decision. Consult is an early exploration of possibilities where you are genuinely listening before considering options. Co-creating means that you are engaging in full partnership. It is the closest stage to pure coaching.

At work, coaching can be used in combination with other stages. Tell (stage 1) and then co-create (stage 5) can be a useful combination. A charity manager with responsibility for encouraging people to give money was preparing an intervention with a local branch that was not paying its way. His plan was that at the end of an evening with him, they would know why it was important to give. He came to a day where we were introducing coaching and realised immediately that his plan had been to sell (stage 2) them the idea that giving was important. Instead, he used tell and co-create. This enabled them all to have two good hours to explore together how they could manage their finances differently. At the end of the evening, they had new insights and were on the way to a plan.

Skilled managers and leaders change hats seamlessly. This ability to be a chameleon and inhabit different roles is very useful. Except when it is confusing.

Changing hats works most effectively when it is done clearly and with consent. '*You can tell he has been on a course because when he comes back to the office, he does it to us for a few days, and then we all get back to normal*', commented someone whose manager had been on a coaching course. Brené Brown says that '*Clear is kind. Unclear is unkind*'.[7] We don't know how to have a great conversation with someone else unless we ask them. And then if we need to change mode, we need to change hats with consent.

If coaching is a different kind of conversation from managing, mentoring, supervising, etc., it is useful to indicate that difference in how we start a conversation, and even where we sit or stand.

Induction and management development programmes

A co-created container can improve the quality of induction, training or development.

People are signed off from a probationary or training period when they can do what they need to do and know what they need to know. Flourishing – for them and the organisation – is about how they do what they do. Starting with the end in mind enables development to be addressed in partnership, in exactly the same way as coaching over time (Fig. 19).

Figure 19 Development programmes

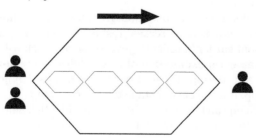

The example I will use here is fantasy and illustrates the difference between transactional and transformational development. In the Church of England, trainee vicars are signed off as ready to have their own parish when they have met a list of competencies including being able to do funerals, weddings and a huge list of other things. Whether life in their new parish is life-giving for them and their community is based on an entirely different list. Imagine that the trainee is very shy and doesn't appear to mix much. Co-creating a contract at the beginning of their training post might sound like:

> 'How will you know six months into your first post after training that this role is life-giving for you? How will the parish know?'

Co-creating also enables you to contribute to the contract.

> 'The organisation will know because we will have ticked off the competencies you need to know. And I'll know because we will see you being sociable enough to fulfil your role'.

Three months into a three-year contract, we meet for a supervision session. Many things will be covered. One will be re-contracting:

> 'Where are we? What's going well? What do we need to focus on? I notice that you have not left the house yet. What do we need to work on here so that by the end of this training you feel confident enough to socialise?'

Notice how this shares responsibility for development. This is different from the person responsible for training turning the gap into a problem and then a performance management issue by involving other stakeholders and beginning to see how to fix the problem. Sharing responsibility for development is partnership.

Even at the last review, if they have still not left the house, this can still be explored in partnership:

> 'I notice that you have not left the house yet and we have three months left of the training. What's the conversation we need to be having?'

This is fantasy, and I hope that it makes the point. Now you can make it your own in your context.

Example of a management development programme

Before the MDP starts:

Their input:

S: 'What do you want to work on in the programme?'

> **T/O:** *'What do you want to be different by the time you finish the programme?'*
> **K:** *'How will we know you've achieved that?'*
> **R:** *'How will you approach the programme to get the most out of it? What support do you need from me?'*
>
> Your input:
> **S:** *'In addition, here's what I'd like you to work on'.*
> **T/O:** *'I expect X to be different by the time you finish the programme'.*
> **K:** *'We'll know you've achieved that by ...'*
> **R:** *'I commit to supporting you by ...'*

Line managers

In a line manager role where you both have things to bring to the conversation, you can still use the coaching container. The contracting process is subtly different. Co-creating the container with STOKeRS is now about bringing in their stuff and yours. There are a number of roles you could take:

- you telling them some things
- them reporting some things
- you helping them think some things through
- you offering ideas or advice

Asking *'How are we going to do this?'* at the start of every conversation achieves two objectives. First, you are able to work out how to do which bits of the conversation differently. That clarity is useful. Second, you are making it clear that how you have the conversation is negotiable. This means that when you check in and ask *'Is this useful?'*, the thinker understands that they can say no and you can together work out a different way of having the conversation.

Example

Manager: *'How do you want to use our one-to-one today?'* (Subject)

Colleague: *'I want to talk about a, b, c'.*

Manager: *'And I would also like us to talk about x, y, z. What do we want to be different around these by the end of this conversation?'* (Their outcome)

Colleague: responds

Manager: *'How will we know we have done that?'* (They'll know)

Colleague: responds

Manager: *'And I would like us to have got to ...'* (Your outcome and how you'll know)

> Manager: *'It sounds like some of this is information sharing, some is advice, and maybe I can enable you to think some of them through'.* (Role)
> Colleague: responds
> Manager: *'Where shall we start?'*

Contracting in a conversation with a direct report is slightly different from an agenda-driven meeting because you will re-contract after each bit.

Check in regularly: *'Is this useful?'* And at each crossroads, ask the thinker: *'Have we finished that bit? What do we need to do next? How shall we do this?'* You are the line manager. Sometimes you will need to decide and tell them how you are going to do some parts of the conversation.

Coaching does not work well if you need to do more than 50 per cent tell in a conversation. Your colleague needs to have enough trust in you for coaching to work. You also need to have enough trust in them. If you are not able to work at that level of partnership, coaching will not be useful.

You wear many hats with colleagues. You are their line manager, you might also be their supervisor, and their friend – or not. It is difficult to manage different roles without a clear boundary. One way to manage this is to have the different conversations in different places, or at least in different chairs. Moving is an efficient way of changing hats. In our office, we do business as usual work in the meeting room and strategy in a local coffee shop for precisely that reason.

Appraisal/review

Appraisal and review evoke mixed feelings. When they work well, they are a transformational developmental tool and serve the individual and the organisation. And sometimes they are a time-consuming transaction. When colleagues fill out paperwork, it can feel like they are writing a draft of the book of the last year. They then come to a conversation with you which ratifies or investigates what they have written. This encounter can feel like a repeat of the paperwork, almost making a film of the book they have already written in real-time. And then one of you writes up the final report. This becomes the review of the film of the book. Little might be known by the person being reviewed at the end of this process that they didn't know when they started their paperwork.

The container can help in appraisals. This requires you to co-create the face-to-face part of the process – and not replicate the process they have already begun. If you completed some 360-degree feedback, you will also have some things that you want to say. Bearing that in mind, you may want to co-create the container and put in some things to talk about. This will look like the line management example above.

Example: 'You've filled in your paperwork. What do you know now that you didn't know before?'
'What do we need to do together today, so you will know that this review will be useful to you (and the organisation) in one (or five) years' time?'
'What's the best way for us to do this today?'
'Where shall we start?'

And then check-in by re-contracting regularly.

Example: 'Is this useful?'
'We have X time left. What do we need to do differently to make this conversation even more useful?'

SOGI can help you keep an eye on the system.

Example: 'How do your intentions fit with those of your team/organisation (or yours with theirs)?'

Instead of using words to step back and take a look in appraisal, changing the medium might give you both a different view. This might look like physically stepping back by standing in the past year and looking at the present, standing in the future and looking at the past, or standing with stakeholders and looking in different places. However you change the medium, be normal about it. Use cups, paper clips, moving or anything that works for you. The segue might simply be: 'Shall we map that out?'

If some written output is required, Clutterbuck and Megginson's Four I's[8] (see Chapter 6) can be useful. This can even be written together in the room.

Coaching up

STOKeRS is a useful framework for a conversation with someone in a more senior position. Rightsizing your question will enable you to have a more effective and efficient conversation

Example: 'I'd like to talk to you about X'.
Becomes: 'You probably have some things you want to talk about. It would be useful for me if we could talk about X (Subject). My question is Y, and it would be great if by the end of this, we had done Y (TOK).'

Meetings

Coaching is about doing some useful work together. Great meetings do useful work, and some of the principles of coaching can be useful. Rightsizing agenda items is useful:

Example

'*By the time we finish this meeting, we need to be clear on ...*' (OUTCOME)
'*We will know that we have moved this on because ...*' (KNOW)
'*So in this (TIME) this is the bit of the thing we are doing*'.
'*This is how we will do it*'. (ROLE – Senge's continuum is useful here)
'*Let's (START HERE) ...*'

In one-to-ones, we learn to notice what is happening and to name that without knowing what to do next. In meetings, participants notice what is going on and don't name it out loud because they don't know what to do next. Drawing from the coaching toolkit simply requires that someone names it. Then the group can work out together what to do next.

> '*How does what we are talking about serve what we are here to do?*'
> '*Who is doing the work?*'
> Name headlines and/or process: '*I'm noticing we are going round in circles here. We seem to be talking about x, y, z. What do we need to do now to get to (OUTCOME)?*'

Introducing movement or changing the medium in meetings can enable the thinker to operate differently. And contracting on actions can add rigour:

> '*How are we going to take this forward? Who?*'
> '*What does that need to look like?*'
> '*How will we know we have done what we agreed over time?*'

Health consultation

Health consultations can be managed in exactly the same way. Using a coaching style is all about enabling the other person to take responsibility for their own health. It also encourages the patient to start from where they are now, rather than going back to the start of their medical history.

Example: STOKeRS

S: '*We are here today to talk about your wellbeing/specific health issue*'.
T: '*We have ten minutes together*'.
O: '*What would you like to leave here with today?*'
K: '*We will know we have been successful when we have identified the next step to stay healthy/maintain/improve your current wellbeing*'.

> **R:** *'Can I suggest you tell me what makes your health an issue today?'*
> **S:** *'Where do we need to start?'*

My colleague Sam Walker regularly uses a coaching style with patients who are regularly readmitted to hospital. She asks questions that are in the present like:

- 'What gets in the way of using your medication/equipment?' Notice the difference between this and a question that asks 'why aren't you taking your medication?'
- 'What do you notice about your visits to the service?'
- 'What is missing to support you staying at home for longer?'
- 'Who do you know that can give you more time to think this through?'

Ending a consultation well also leaves responsibility in the right place:

C – *'So you wanted X. Where are you with that now?'*
A – *'This is what I will do for you today. What will be your next step?'*
L – *'What do you know now that you didn't know before?'*
F – *'Are we done?'*

If more time is needed the thinker can be offered an appointment to an appropriate service.

Social prescribing

Social prescribing is a new role in the UK's National Health Service designed to support patients who need community interaction. Patients are referred to link workers or social prescribers for a conversation. The name sounds like the prescriber will be offering a treatment. If these conversations are going to have a sustained impact, they will need to look and feel different from other conversations that the person has had with medical professionals. For social prescribing to work, patients will need to take action as a result of the conversation that will make a difference to them. It is coaching.

> **Ruth's Story**
>
> Working in a consulting room of a surgery, I saw a man for a first session. He was struggling with how to find a way forward with managing at home. He was hoarding and well and truly stuck in the clutter, feeling helpless and overwhelmed. We rightsized the work and agreed that by the end of the

session he would make a plan so that he could go home and make a start. As we spoke, it was evident that the stuckness felt quite physical. We sat in the consulting room chairs, his motivation was low, and any thoughts of options moving forward were proving hard to find.

I offered that we could try something different if he agreed. I suggested we stand and 'look at the situation' and by looking at it, see if there were more options. As we stood together in the imaginary space that was the chaos at home, the man was instantly more energised and focused. He began to speak with animation and determination. Talking about where he could start and what needed to happen, we pointed into the imaginary mess at what could be possible options. He became unstuck. When he was done, we sat again, and I asked if we needed to do anything further. Did he need to commit this plan to paper? He said that wouldn't be necessary as he was confident he had a plan and knew what he wanted to do. In the follow-up session we did a quick review, and although he did not do exactly what he had said in session one, he did make a real start that day and is still enjoying the benefits that brought.

People who are dying and grieving

Don Eisenhauer,[9] a coach in the USA, does all his coaching with people who are dying or grieving. The stance that people are robust enough to deal with their own stuff can be life-affirming. The need for coaching people who are grieving has become more acute through the Covid-19 pandemic, which has brought some kind of loss to almost everyone across the world. A coaching style of enabling someone to feel heard without needing to fix or minimise is needed more now than ever before.

A friend of mine sadly died as I was writing this book. Towards the end she could only tolerate very short visits. On my last visit, I said '*We have five minutes?*' She used them to excitedly tell me that she had found a safe home for her precious violin and how delighted she was that now she could die in peace. This was not a conversation I was expecting to have and is a great example of the value of rightsizing.

Coaching in schools

Across education, a style of coaching is used with teachers who are perceived to be underperforming. This commonly sounds like Senge's tell: '*To get this grade you will need to do a, b, c*'. This is transactional. Partnership with teachers who are perceived to be underperforming is more transformational and might look like this. (This works best if you are not in the seating position where they are expecting to be told what to do. Walking or standing can help because you can move):

> *'It feels like this is where you are now'.* [Move] *'Here we are, and you are confident, and you're getting better results and great feedback'.*
> *'Is that what you want?'*
> *'Standing here and looking back, what are the things that need to be in place to enable that to happen?'*
> *'What's your role? My role? The school's role, in supporting you to get there?'*

Teachers I work with in schools use the principles described in this book without calling it coaching. A coaching style is an opportunity to give a voice and time to be heard to support staff who have not been heard for a long time, and don't believe they have the language to communicate what they want to say. Teacher Sarah Clarke describes this as 'opening a box of confidence'. Colleagues who need to deliver on strategic priorities talk to an external coach. The headteacher checks in on the effectiveness of coaching asking colleagues: 'How effective is coaching in supporting you with what you want and need to do?' In this way, coaching becomes about the quality of the vehicle for improvement and how people engage with the process and not about how effective the people are. 'The more we can trust the process, the more autonomy and trust we build with our colleagues', says Sarah.

A behaviour support assistant said:

> *'I have felt more capable of having difficult conversations, I've been more able to slow down interactions and realise that the time I invest is worthwhile as it pays off in the long run or I've been able to steer a conversation/ interaction and keep it on point. For example, a conversation with the parent where I may find the parent goes off topic, I've been able to pull that back into topic much easier without feeling that I am being rude. With students, I have used it dealing with medical and behavioural issues'.*

A Support Teacher's Story

When a student wants to talk, I will ask if they are able to wait and speak out of lesson time. If they say they cannot wait, then I will stipulate I have five minutes (so that they are not using time as an excuse to miss lessons). I will ensure that I stay quiet as they speak, something that I have found difficult to do in the past, particularly when they are complaining about members of staff.

I will encourage the student to solve their problems themselves. I will ask them to speak to the teachers concerned rather than expecting me to go and sort things for them. I now recognise that students should be sorting issues themselves rather than going around multiple members of staff and playing staff off against each other. This is going to make them more resilient. If they resolve their issues, there is no need for other members of staff to become involved, undermining others and overriding sanctions given.

A coaching style works across organisations. It enables people to feel heard and gain new insights. Let's leave the last word to a headteacher:

'Coaching has been invaluable to me as a senior leader as it has given me dedicated time and space to just stop, reflect, acknowledge what has been achieved and what the priorities are moving forward. Coaching gives clarity to my thoughts and re-energises me. The main impact for me is that by investing in a forty-five-minute coaching session I can gain back hours where I might have been mulling something over'.

Notes

1   Karpman, S. (1968), *Fairy tales and script drama analysis*, available at: www.karpmandramatriangle.com/pdf/DramaTriangle.pdf (accessed 27 March 2020).
2   https://keithwebb.com with permission.
3   Engelmann, J., Capra, C., Noussair, C. and Berns, G. (2009), *Given 'expert advice', brains shut down*, available at: www.wired.com/2009/03/financebrain/ (accessed 27 March 2020).
4   Hawkins, P. and Smith, N. (2013), *Coaching, Mentoring and Organizational Consultancy: Supervision, Skills and Development*, 2nd edition, Maidenhead: Open University Press.
5   YouTube (2018), *Meet the artist leaving positive notes to strangers around London*, available at: https://youtu.be/FJbTD_Zgtmk (accessed 1 April 2020).
6   Senge, P. (2006), *The Fifth Discipline: The Art and Practice of the Learning Organization*, revised edition, London: Doubleday.
7   Brown, B. (2018), *Dare to Lead: Bold Work. Tough Conversations. Whole Hearts*, London: Vermilion.
8   Clutterbuck, D. and Megginson, D. (2016), *Techniques for Coaching and Mentoring*, 2nd edition, London: Routledge.
9   Eisenhauer, D. and Hastings, J.V. (2013), *Coaching at End of Life: A Coach Approach to Ministering to the Dying and the Grieving*, USA: Coaching at End of Life.

9 The journey continues

Is the coach the pilot, the air traffic controller or a fellow passenger? It doesn't matter as long as our work is travelling together with the thinker in a way that serves them and their context. Thinkers leave their conversations with us moving forward into their future. In the same way, your journey continues as you finish this book. '*To make an end*' says T.S. Eliot,[1] '*is to make a beginning. We shall not cease from exploration, and the end of our exploring will be to arrive where we started and know the place for the first time*'. My hope is that this book has given you some insights that will make the conversations you have more useful to the people with whom you work. And that you will continue to learn and to simplify.

'*The only way to learn mathematics is to do mathematics*' says Paul Halmos.[2] The only way to become an outstanding coach is to do coaching. Coaching is much more about behaviour than it is about knowledge. And you will never do it perfectly. In coaching at all levels, when the process is working for them, the thinker will rarely remember your questions, unless they are ones they need to continue to ponder. They will remember the learning.

When they see the container for the first time, I often hear people comment that the work must be shallow. People will go as deep as they want to go. And sometimes they go deep fast. Although I have used here the metaphor of a plane, the lozenge could equally be a submarine going down deep for the conversation and emerging back to the surface at the conversation's end.

If coaching is your main profession, working with a mentor coach on developing lightness in the room is as important as working with a supervisor on your self-reflection. Make sure your mentor coach listens with you to recordings of your coaching. Use the learning lab of the coaching room as much as you use your library of books and courses.

Simplifying Coaching could be called *The Book of Tweaks*. I encourage you to apply one piece of learning at a time so that you don't overwhelm those with whom you work! Simplifying coaching is about improving the quality of our conversations in service of those with whom we talk. Stop working so hard. Make the language work in your context. And keep it simple!

Working simply is about acknowledging the power we have, being clear and straight about it and not letting it get in the way. Coaching is about two human beings doing deep work lightly: *'Take off your shoes – the place you are standing is holy ground'*.[3]

Notes

1   Eliot, T.S. (1943), *Four Quartets*, New York: Harcourt, Brace.
2   Halmos, P.R., Moise, E.E. and Piranian, G. (1975), 'The problem of learning to teach', *The American Mathematical Monthly*, 82 (5): 466–476, available at: www.jstor.org/stable/2319737 (accessed 2 April 2020).
3   *Holy Bible – New International Version* (1986), London: Hodder & Stoughton.

Further reading

Some of the following are coaching books. Some are books that have inspired me and where you can make your own meaning.

Bloom, P. (2018), *Against Empathy*, New York: Vintage Books.

Bryson, B. (2019), *The Body: A Guide for Occupants*, London: Doubleday.

Covey, S. and Merrill, R. (2008), *The Speed of Trust: The One Thing that Changes*, London: Simon & Schuster.

David, S., Clutterbuck, D. and Megginson, D., (2016), *Beyond Goals*, Abingdon: Routledge.

Eddo-Lodge, R. (2018), *Why I'm No Longer Talking to White People about Race*, London: Bloomsbury.

Eliot, T.S. (2002), *Collected Poems 1909–62*, London: Faber & Faber.

Schein, E. and Pratt, S., (2013), *Humble Inquiry: The Gentle Art of Asking Instead of Telling*, San Francisco, CA: Berrett-Koehler.

Index